Oscar Fingal O'Flahertie Wills Wilde (16 October 1854 – 30 November 1900) was an Irish poet and playwright. After writing in different forms throughout the 1880s, he became one of London's most popular playwrights in the early 1890s. He is best remembered for his epigrams and plays, his novel The Picture of Dorian Gray, and the circumstances of his criminal conviction for homosexuality, imprisonment, and early death at age 46. Wilde's parents were successful Anglo-Irish intellectuals in Dublin. Their son became fluent in French and German early in life. At university, Wilde read Greats; he proved himself to be an outstanding classicist, first at Trinity College Dublin, then at Oxford. He became known for his involvement in the rising philosophy of aestheticism, led by two of his tutors, Walter Pater and John Ruskin. After university, Wilde moved to London into fashionable cultural and social circles. (Source: Wikipedia)

Literary works:
Ravenna (1878)
Poems (1881)
The Happy Prince and Other Stories (1888)
Lord Arthur Savile's Crime and Other Stories (1891)
A House of Pomegranates (1891)
Intentions (1891)
The Picture of Dorian Gray (1890)
The Soul of Man under Socialism (1891)
Lady Windermere's Fan (1892)
A Woman of No Importance (1893)
An Ideal Husband (1898)
The Importance of Being Earnest (1898)
De Profundis (1905)
The Ballad of Reading Gaol (1898)
The Portrait of Mr. W. H. (1889)

MISCELLANEOUS APHORISMS
Oscar Wilde

PRINCE CLASSICS

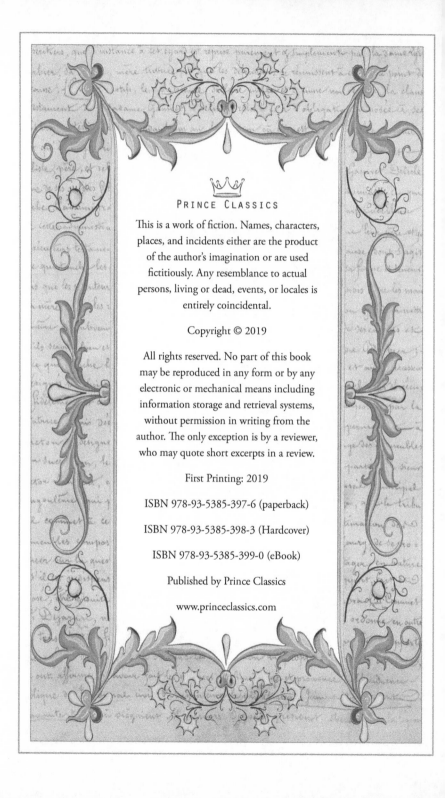

PRINCE CLASSICS

First Printing: 2019

ISBN 978-93-5385-397-6 (paperback)

ISBN 978-93-5385-398-3 (Hardcover)

ISBN 978-93-5385-399-0 (eBook)

Published by Prince Classics

www.princeclassics.com

Contents

MISCELLANEOUS APHORISMS

SEBASTIAN MELMOTH

(OSCAR WILDE)

The mystery of love is greater than the mystery of death.

Women are made to be loved, not to be understood.

It is absurd to have a hard and fast rule about what one should read and what one shouldn't. Moren than half of modern culture depends on what one shouldn't read.

Women, as someone says, love with their ears, just as men love with their eyes, if they ever love at all.

It is better to be beautiful than to be good, but it is better to be good than to be ugly.

Nothing looks so like innocence as an indiscretion.

Misfortunes one can endure, they come from outside, they are accidents. But to suffer for one's faults—ah! there is the sting of life.

Beauty is the only thing that time cannot harm. Philosophies fall away like sand, creeds follow one another, but what is beautiful is a joy for all seasons, a possession for all eternity.

Questions are never indiscreet; answers sometimes are.

Twenty years of romance make a woman look like a ruin; but twenty years of marriage make her something like a public building.

The only thing that one really knows about human nature is that it changes.

Anyone can sympathise with the sufferings of a friend, but it requires a very fine nature to sympathise with a friend's success.

Selfishness is not living as one wishes to live, it is asking others to live as one wishes to live: and unselfishness is letting other people's lives alone, not interfering with them.

A man who does not think for himself does not think at all.

Nowadays people seem to look on life as a speculation. It is not a speculation. It is a sacrament. Its ideal is love. Its purification is sacrifice.

In old days nobody pretended to be a bit better than his neighbour. In fact, to be a bit better than one's neighbour was considered excessively vulgar and middle class. Nowadays, with our modern mania for morality, everyone has to pose as a paragon of purity, incorruptibility, and all the other seven deadly virtues. And what is the result? You all go over like ninepins—one after the other.

All sympathy is fine, but sympathy with suffering is the least fine mode.

If you pretend to be good the world takes you very seriously. If you pretend to be bad it doesn't. Such is the astounding stupidity of optimism.

It is most dangerous nowadays for a husband to pay any attention to his wife in public. It always makes people think that he beats her when they're alone. The world has grown so suspicious of anything that looks like a happy married life.

Actors are so fortunate. They can choose whether they will appear in tragedy or in comedy, whether they will suffer or make merry, laugh or shed tears. But in real life it is different. Most men and women are forced to perform parts for which they have no qualifications. The world is a stage, but the play is badly cast.

Men know life too early; women know life too late-that is the difference between men and women.

He who stands most remote from his age is he who mirrors it best.

There is only one thing in the world worse than being talked about, and that is not being talked about.

Life is not governed by will or intention. Life is a question of nerves and fibres and slowly built-up cells, in which thought hides itself and passion has its dreams.

Man is a being with myriad lives and myriad sensations, a complex, multiform creature that bears within itself strange legacies of thought and passion, and whose very flesh is tainted with the monstrous maladies of the dead.

As long as a woman can look ten years younger than her own daughter she is perfectly satisfied.

There is always something infinitely mean about other people's tragedies.

Public and private life are different things. They have different laws and move on different lines.

When one is placed in the position of guardian one has to adopt a very high moral tone on all subjects. It's one's duty to do so.

I have always been of opinion that a man who desires to get married should know either everything or nothing.

An engagement should come on a young girl as a surprise, pleasant or unpleasant, as the case may be. It is hardly a matter that she could be allowed to arrange for herself.

If the lower classes don't set us a good example what on earth is the use of them? They seem, as a class, to have absolutely no sense of moral responsibility.

If a woman cannot make her mistakes charming she is only a female.

The world was made for men and not for women.

It is always with the best intentions that the worst work is done.

If you wish to understand others you must intensify your own individualism.

Why do you talk so trivially about life? Because I think that life is far too important a thing ever to talk seriously about it.

What a pity that in life we only get our lessons when they are of no use to us.

It is better to have a permanent income than to be fascinating.

Relations are simply a tedious pack of people who haven't got the remotest knowledge of how to live nor the smallest instinct about when to die.

Charity creates a multitude of sins.

My experience is that as soon as people are old enough to know better they don't know anything at all.

Truth is a very complex thing and politics is a very complex business. There are wheels within wheels. One may be under certain obligations to people that one must pay. Sooner or later in political life one has to compromise. Everyone does.

Men can love what is beneath them—things unworthy, stained, dishonoured. We women worship when we love; and when we lose our worship we lose everything.

The proper basis for marriage is a mutual misunderstanding.

The one advantage of playing with fire is that one never gets even singed. It is the people who don't know how to play with it who get burned up.

There are moments when one has to choose between living one's own life fully, entirely, completely, or dragging out some false, shallow, degrading existence that the world in its hypocrisy demands.

When one is in town one amuses oneself. When one is in the country one amuses other people. It is excessively boring.

Romance is the privilege of the rich, not the profession of the unemployed. The poor should be practical and prosaic.

An acquaintance that begins with a compliment is sure to develop into a real friendship. It starts in the right manner.

The truths of metaphysics are the truths of masks.

Science can never grapple with the irrational. That is why it has no future before it in this world.

The happy people of the world have their value, but only the negative value of foils. They throw up and emphasise the beauty and the fascination of the unhappy.

In this world there are only two tragedies. One is not getting what one wants, and the other is getting it. The last is much the worst—the last is a real tragedy.

Disobedience in the eyes of anyone who has read history is man's original virtue. It is through disobedience that progress has been made—through disobedience and rebellion.

It is not wise to find symbols in everything that one sees. It makes life too full of terrors.

Comfort is the only thing our civilisation can give us.

Politics are my only pleasure. You see nowadays it is not fashionable to flirt till one is forty or to be romantic till one is forty-five, so we poor women who are under thirty, or say we are, have nothing open to us but politics or philanthropy. And philanthropy seems to me to have become simply the refuge of people who wish to annoy their fellow-creatures. I prefer politics. I think they are more ... becoming.

One's past is what one is. It is the only way by which people should be judged.

In a very ugly and sensible age the arts borrow, not from life, but from each other.

It is always a silly thing to give advice, but to give good advice is fatal.

Secrets from other people's wives are a necessary luxury in modern life.

So, at least, I am told at the club by people who are bald enough to know better. But no man should have a secret from his own wife. She invariably finds it out. Women have a wonderful instinct about things. They discover everything except the obvious.

Life holds the mirror up to art, and either reproduces some strange type imagined by painter or sculptor or realises in fact what has been dreamed in fiction.

I feel sure that if I lived in the country for six months I should become so unsophisticated that no one would take the slightest notice of me.

To recommend thrift to the poor is both grotesque and insulting. It is like advising a man who is starving to eat less.

A thing is not necessarily true because a man dies for it.

I am always saying what I shouldn't say; in fact, I usually say what I really think—a great mistake nowadays. It makes one so liable to be misunderstood.

Experience is the name everyone gives to their mistakes.

The true perfection of man lies, not in what man has, but in what man is.

The basis of every scandal is an absolute immoral certainty.

People talk so much about the beauty of confidence. They seem to entirely ignore the much more subtle beauty of doubt. To believe is very dull. To doubt is intensely engrossing. To be on the alert is to live, to be lulled into security is to die.

Every effect that one produces gives one an enemy. To be popular one must be a mediocrity.

It is a sad truth, but we have lost the faculty of giving lovely names to things. Names are everything. I never quarrel with actions, my one quarrel is with words. That is the reason I hate vulgar realism in literature. The man who could call a spade a spade should be compelled to use one. It is the only thing he is fit for.

14

A high moral tone can hardly be said to conduce very much to either one's health or one's happiness.

There are terrible temptations that it requires strength—strength and courage—to yield to. To stake all one's life on one throw—whether the stake be power or pleasure I care not—there is no weakness in that. There is a horrible, a terrible, courage.

Nowadays it is only the unreadable that occurs.

All charming people are spoiled. It is the secret of their attraction.

There is more to be said for stupidity than people imagine. Personally, I have a great admiration for stupidity. It is a sort of fellow-feeling, I suppose.

All men are monsters. The only thing to do is to feed the wretches well. A good cook does wonders.

There is no such thing as an omen.

Destiny does not send us heralds. She is too wise or too cruel for that.

Crying is the refuge of plain women but the ruin of pretty ones.

Love art for its own sake and then all things that you need will be added to you. This devotion to beauty and to the creation of beautiful things is the test of all great civilisations; it is what makes the life of each citizen a sacrament and not a speculation.

It is always worth while asking a question, though it is not always answering one.

It takes a thoroughly good woman to do a thoroughly stupid thing.

With a proper background women can do anything.

Chiromancy is a most dangerous science, and one that ought not to be encouraged, except in a 'tête-à-tête.'

One should never take sides in anything. Taking sides is the beginning of sincerity, and earnestness follows shortly afterwards, and the human being becomes a bore.

The work of art is beautiful by being what art never has been; and to measure it by the standard of the past is to measure it by a standard on the reflection of which its real perfection depends.

There are three kinds of despots. There is the despot who tyrannises over the body. There is the despot who tyrannises over the soul. There is the despot who tyrannises over soul and body alike. The first is called the prince. The second is called the pope. The third is called the people.

Costume is a growth, an evolution, and a most important, perhaps the most important, sign of the manners, customs, and mode of life of each century.

I really don't see anything romantic in proposing. It is very romantic to be in love, but there is nothing romantic about a definite proposal. Why, one may be accepted. One usually is, I believe. Then the excitement is all over. The very essence of romance is uncertainty.

What consoles one nowadays is not repentance but pleasure. Repentance is quite out of date.

Ideals are dangerous things. Realities are better. They wound, but they are better.

Unless one is wealthy there is no use in being a charming fellow.

Shallow sorrows and shallow loves live on. The loves and sorrows that are great are destroyed by their own plenitude.

An eternal smile is much more wearisome than a perpetual frown. The one sweeps away all possibilities, the other suggests a thousand.

To disagree with three-fourths of England on all points is one of the first elements of vanity, which is a deep source of consolation in all moments of spiritual doubt.

Women live by their emotions and for them, they have no philosophy of life.

16

As long as war is regarded as wicked it will always have a fascination. When it is looked upon as vulgar it will cease to be popular.

There is only one thing worse than injustice, and that is justice without her sword in her hand. When right is not might it is evil.

We spend our days, each one of us, in looking for the secret of life. Well, the secret of life is in art.

The truth isn't quite the sort of thing that one tells to a nice, sweet, refined girl.

If one plays good music people don't listen, and if one plays bad music people don't talk.

How fond women are of doing dangerous things. It is one of the qualities in them that I admire most. A woman will flirt with anybody in the world as long as other people are looking on.

Englishwomen conceal their feelings till after they are married. They show them then.

Moderation is a fatal thing. Nothing succeeds like excess.

Actions are the first tragedy in life, words are the second. Words are perhaps the worst. Words are merciless.

Life is terrible. It rules us, we do not rule it.

In art there is no such thing as a universal truth. A truth in art is that whose contradictory is also true.

One's days are too brief to take the burden of another's sorrows on one's shoulders. Each man lives his own life, and pays his own price for living it. The only pity is that one has to pay so often for a single fault. One has to pay over and over again, indeed. In her dealings with man Destiny never closes her accounts.

Pleasure is Nature's test, her sign of approval. When we are happy we are always good, but when we are good we are not always happy.

The people who love only once in their lives are really the shallow people. What they call their loyalty and their fidelity I call either the lethargy of custom or their lack of imagination.

Better to take pleasure in a rose than to put its root under a microscope.

Of Shakespeare it may be said that he was the first to see the dramatic value of doublets and that a climax may depend on a crinoline.

Plain women are always jealous of their husbands; beautiful women never are! They never have time. They are always so occupied in being jealous of other people's husbands.

What between the duties expected of one during one's lifetime and the duties exacted from one after one's death land has ceased to be either a profit or a pleasure. It gives one position and prevents one from keeping it up.

A man who moralises is usually a hypocrite, and a woman who moralises is invariably plain. There is nothing in the whole world so unbecoming to a woman as a nonconformist conscience. And most women know it, I am glad to say.

It was a fatal day when the public discovered that the pen is mightier than the paving-stone and can be made as offensive as a brickbat.

A map of the world that does not include Utopia is not worth even glancing at, for it leaves out the one country at which Humanity is always landing. And when Humanity lands there it looks out, and, seeing a better country, sets sail. Progress is the realisation of Utopias.

What is the difference between scandal and gossip? Oh! gossip is charming! History is merely gossip, but scandal is gossip made tedious by morality.

All beautiful things belong to the same age.

It is personalities, not principles, that move the age.

Modern pictures are, no doubt, delightful to look at. At least, some of them are. But they are quite impossible to live with; they are too clever, too assertive, too intellectual. Their meaning is too obvious and their method too clearly defined. One exhausts what they have to say in a very short time, and then they become as tedious as one's relations.

To know nothing about our great men is one of the necessary elements of English education.

The truth is rarely pure and never simple. Modern life would be very tedious if it were either and modern literature a complete impossibility.

You may laugh, but it is a great thing to come across a woman who thoroughly understands one.

The majority of people spoil their lives by an unhealthy and exaggerated altruism.

The number of women in London who flirt with their own husbands is perfectly scandalous. It looks so bad. It is simply washing one's clean linen in public.

The chief thing that makes life a failure from the artistic point of view is the thing that lends to life its sordid security—the fact that one can never repeat exactly the same emotion.

We teach people how to remember, we never teach them how to grow.

Vulgar habit that is people have nowadays of asking one, after one has given them an idea, whether one is serious or not. Nothing is serious except passion. The intellect is not a serious thing and never has been. It is an instrument on which one plays, that is all. The only serious form of intellect I know is the British intellect, and on the British intellect the illiterate always plays the drum.

It is absurd to divide people into good and bad. People are either charming or tedious.

It is only the modern that ever become old-fashioned.

It is only the Philistine who seeks to estimate a personality by the vulgar test of production.

Musical people are so absurdly unreasonable. They always want one to be perfectly dumb at the very moment when one is longing to be absolutely deaf.

Nothing is so dangerous as being too modern. One is apt to grow old-fashioned quite suddenly.

The fact of a man being a poisoner is nothing against his prose. The domestic virtues are not the true basis of art.

To the philosopher women represent the triumph of matter over mind, just as men represent the triumph of mind over morals.

The only way a woman can ever reform a man is by boring him so completely that he loses all possible interest in life.

The only horrible thing in the world is 'ennui.' That is the one sin for which there is no forgiveness.

French songs I cannot possibly allow. People always seem to think that they are improper, and either look shocked, which is vulgar, or laugh, which is worse.

It has often been made a subject of reproach against artists and men of letters that they are lacking in wholeness and completeness of nature. As a rule this must necessarily be so. That very concentration of vision and inversity of purpose which is the characteristic of the artistic temperament is in itself a mode of limitation. To those who are preoccupied with the beauty of form nothing else seems of so much importance.

The work of art is to dominate the spectator. The spectator is not to dominate the work of art.

One should sympathise with the joy, the beauty, the colour of life. The less said about life's sores the better.

You can't make people good by act of Parliament—that is something.

Art creates an incomparable and unique effect, and having done so passes on to other things. Nature, on the other hand, forgetting that imitation can be made the sincerest form of insult, keeps on repeating the effect until we all become absolutely wearied of it.

It is perfectly monstrous the way people go about nowadays saying things against one behind one's back that are absolutely and entirely true.

A true artist takes no notice whatever of the public. The public are to him non-existent.

One should never trust a woman who tells one her real age. A woman who would tell one that would tell one anything.

Nothing is so aggravating as calmness. There is something positively brutal about the good temper of most modern men. I wonder we women stand it as well as we do.

The truth is a thing I get rid of as soon as possible. Bad habit, by the way, makes one very unpopular at the club ... with the older members. They call it being conceited. Perhaps it is.

My own business always bores me to death. I prefer other people's.

Don't be led astray into the paths of virtue—that is the worst of women. They always want one to be good. And if we are good, when they meet us they don't love us at all. They like to find us quite irretrievably bad and to leave us quite unattractively good.

Men are such cowards. They outrage every law in the world and are afraid of the world's tongue.

Wicked women bother one. Good women bore one. That is the only difference between them.

To know the principles of the highest art is to know the principles of all the arts.

I don't believe in the existence of Puritan women. I don't think there is a woman in the world who would not be a little flattered if one made love to her. It is that which makes women so irresistibly adorable.

When I am in trouble eating is the only thing that consoles me. Indeed,

21

when I am in really great trouble, as anyone who knows me intimately will tell you, I refuse everything except food and drink.

When one is going to lead an entirely new life one requires regular and wholesome meals.

The soul is born old, but grows young. That is the comedy of life. The body is born young, and grows old. That is life's tragedy.

One can survive everything nowadays except death, and live down anything except a good reputation.

The past is of no importance. The present is of no importance. It is with the future that we have to deal. For the past is what men should not have been. The present is what men ought not to be. The future is what artists are.

Men become old, but they never become good.

By persistently remaining single a man converts himself into a permanent public temptation. Men should be more careful; this very celibacy leads weaker vessels astray.

I think that in practical life there is something about success, actual success, that is a little unscrupulous, something about ambition that is scrupulous always.

Every man of ambition has to fight his century with its own weapons. What this century worships is wealth. The god of this century is wealth. To succeed one must have wealth. At all costs one must have wealth.

I love scandals about other people, but scandals about myself don't interest me. They have not got the charm of novelty.

Moderation is a fatal thing. Enough is as bad as a meal. More than enough is as good as a feast.

The English can't stand a man who is always saying he is in the right, but they are very fond of a man who admits he has been in the wrong. It is one of the best things in them.

Life is simply a 'mauvais quart d'heure' made up of exquisite moments.

There is the same world for all of us, and good and evil, sin and innocence, go through it hand in hand. To shut one's eyes to half of life that one may live securely is as though one blinded oneself that one might walk with more safety in a land of pit and precipice.

Married men are horribly tedious when they are good husbands and abominably conceited when they are not.

Between men and women there is no friendship possible. There is passion, enmity, worship, love, but no friendship.

Everybody is clever nowadays. You can't go anywhere without meeting clever people. This has become an absolute public nuisance.

I don't think man has much capacity for development. He has got as far as he can, and that is not far, is it?

I am not quite sure that I quite know what pessimism really means. All I do know is that life cannot be understood without much charity, cannot be lived without much charity. It is love, and not German philosophy, that is the explanation of this world, whatever may be the explanation of the next.

I do not approve of anything that that tampers with natural arrogance. Ignorance is like a delicate exotic fruit: touch it, and the blossom is gone.

The whole theory of modern education is radically unsound. Fortunately, in England, at any rate, education produces no effect whatsoever. If it did it would prove a serious danger to the upper classes, and probably lead to acts of violence in Grosvenor Square.

No woman should ever be quite accurate about her age. It looks so calculating.

Emotion for the sake of emotion is the aim of art, and emotion for the sake of emotion is the aim of life and of that practical organisation of life that we call society.

Men of the noblest possible moral character are extremely susceptible to the influence of the physical charms of others. Modern, no less than ancient, history supplies us with many most painful examples of what I refer to. If it were not so, indeed, history would be quite unreadable.

I am not in favour of long engagements. They give people the opportunity of finding out each other's character before marriage, which I think is never advisable.

It is a terrible thing for a man to find out suddenly that all his life he has been speaking nothing but the truth.

The two weak points in our age are its want of principle and its want of profile.

Thirty-five is a very attractive age. London society is full of women who have of their own free choice remained thirty-five for years.

Never speak disrespectfully of society. Only people who can't get into it do that.

It is always painful to part with people whom one has known for a very brief space of time. The absence of old friends one can endure with equanimity. But even a momentary separation from anyone to whom one has just been introduced is almost unbearable.

To be natural is to be obvious, and to be obvious is to be inartistic.

One is tempted to define man as a rational animal who always loses his temper when he is called upon to act in accordance with the dictates of reason.

The essence of thought, as the essence of life, is growth.

What people call insincerity is simply a method by which we can multiply our personalities.

In a temple everyone should be serious except the thing that is worshipped.

We are never more true to ourselves than when we are inconsistent.

There is always something ridiculous about the emotions of people whom one has ceased to love.

Intellectual generalities are always interesting, but generalities in morals mean absolutely nothing.

To be in society is merely a bore, but to be out of it simply a tragedy.

We live in an age when unnecessary things are our only necessities.

One should never make one's début with a scandal. One should reserve that to give an interest to one's old age.

What man has sought for is, indeed, neither pain nor pleasure, but simply life. Man has sought to live intensely, fully, perfectly. When he can do so without exercising restraint on others, or suffering it ever, and his activities are all pleasurable to him, he will be saner, healthier, more civilised, more himself. Pleasure is nature's test, her sign of approval. When man is happy he is in harmony with himself and his environment.

Society often forgives the criminal, it never forgives the dreamer.

It is so easy for people to have sympathy with suffering. It is so difficult for them to have sympathy with thought.

Conversation should touch on everything, but should concentrate itself on nothing.

There is a luxury in self-reproach. When we blame ourselves we feel that no one else has a right to blame us. It is the confession, not the priest, that gives us absolution.

There are only two kinds of people who are really fascinating—people who know absolutely everything and people who know absolutely nothing.

The public is wonderfully tolerant; it forgives everything except genius.

Life makes us pay too high a price for its wares, and we purchase the meanest of its secrets at a cost that is monstrous and infinite.

This horrid House of Commons quite ruins our husbands for us. I think the Lower House by far the greatest blow to a happy married life that there has been since that terrible thing they called the Higher Education of Women was invented.

Once a man begins to neglect his domestic duties he becomes painfully effeminate, does he not? And I don't like that. It makes men so very attractive.

Experience is a question of instinct about life.

What is true about art is true about life.

One can always be kind to people about whom one cares nothing.

I like men who have a future and women who have a past.

Women, as some witty Frenchman put it, inspire us with the desire to do masterpieces and always prevent us from carrying them out.

In matters of grave importance style, not sincerity, is the vital thing.

The only way to behave to a woman, is to make love to her if she is pretty and to someone else if she is plain.

Women give to men the very gold of their lives. Possibly; but they invariably want it back in such very small change.

Define women as a sex? Sphinxes without secrets.

What do you call a bad man? The sort of man who admires innocence.

What do you call a bad woman? Oh! the sort of woman a man never gets tired of.

One can resist everything except temptation.

Don't let us go to life for our fulfilment or our experience. It is a thing narrowed by circumstances, incoherent in its utterance, and without that fine correspondence or form and spirit which is the only thing that can satisfy the artistic and critical temperament.

It is a dangerous thing to reform anyone.

One can always know at once whether a man has home claims upon his life or not. I have noticed a very, very sad expression in the eyes of so many married men.

A mother who doesn't part with a daughter every season has no real affection.

To be good is to be in harmony with oneself. Discord is to be forced to be in harmony with others.

A really grand passion is comparatively rare nowadays. It is the privilege of people who have nothing to do. That is the one use of the idle classes in a country.

There is no secret of life. Life's aim, if it has one, is simply to be always looking for temptations. There are not nearly enough of them; I sometimes pass a whole day without coming across a single one. It is quite dreadful. It makes one so nervous about the future.

All thought is immoral. Its very essence is destruction. If you think of anything you kill it; nothing survives being thought of.

What is truth? In matters of religion it is simply the opinion that has survived. In matters of science it is the ultimate sensation. In matters of art it is one's last mood.

It is so easy to convert others. It is so difficult to convert oneself.

A little sincerity is a dangerous thing, and a great deal of it is absolutely fatal.

Life cheats us with shadows, like a puppet-master. We ask it for pleasure. It gives it to us, with bitterness and disappointment in its train. We come across some noble grief that we think will lend the purple dignity of tragedy to our days, but it passes away from us, and things less noble take its place, and on some grey, windy dawn, or odorous eve of silence and of silver, we find ourselves looking with callous wonder, or dull heart of stone, at the tress of gold-flecked hair that we had once so wildly worshipped and so madly kissed.

There are two ways of disliking art One is to dislike it and the other to like it rationally.

There is nothing sane about the worship of beauty. It is too splendid to be sane. Those of whose lives it forms the dominant note will always seem to the world to be mere visionaries.

I am afraid that good people do a great deal of harm in this world. Certainly the greatest harm they do is that they make badness of such extraordinary importance.

A sentimentalist is a man who sees an absurd value in everything and doesn't know the marked price of any single thing.

Punctuality is the thief of time.

Self-culture is the true ideal for man.

There's nothing in the world like the devotion of a married woman. It's a thing no married man knows anything about.

No woman should have a memory. Memory in a woman is the beginning of dowdiness. One can always tell from a woman's bonnet whether she has got a memory or not.

There are things that are right to say but that may be said at the wrong time and to the wrong people.

The meaning of any beautiful created thing is, at least, as much in the soul of him who looks at it as it was in his soul who wrought it. Nay, it is rather the beholder who lends to the beautiful thing its myriad meanings, and makes it marvellous for us, and sets it in some new relation to the age, so that it becomes a vital portion of our lives and a symbol of what we pray for, or perhaps of what, having prayed for, we fear that we may receive.

The Renaissance was great because it sought to solve no social problem, and busied itself not about such things, but suffered the individual to develop freely, beautifully, and naturally, and so had great and individual artists and great and individual men.

In England people actually try to be brilliant at breakfast. That is so dreadful of them! Only dull people are brilliant at breakfast.

When one is in love one begins by deceiving oneself, and one ends by deceiving others. That is what the world calls a romance.

The secret of life is never to have an emotion that is unbecoming.

No artist is ever morbid. The artist can express everything.

The development of the race depends on the development of the individual, and where self-culture has ceased to be the ideal the intellectual standard is instantly lowered and often ultimately lost.

An idea that is not dangerous is unworthy of being called an idea at all.

To elope is cowardly; it is running away from danger, and danger has become so rare in modern life.

When a man is old enough to do wrong he should be old enough to do right also.

The Book of Life begins with a man and a woman in a garden. It ends with Revelations.

In married life three is company and two is none.

Out of ourselves we can never pass, nor can there be in creation what in the creator was not.

Don't tell me that you have exhausted life. When a man says that one knows that life has exhausted him.

When a woman marries again it is because she detested her first husband. When a man marries again it is because he adored his first wife. Women try their luck; men risk theirs.

The highest criticism really is the record of one's own soul. It is more fascinating than history, as it is concerned simply with oneself. It is more delightful than philosophy, as its subject is concrete and not abstract, real and not vague. It is the only civilised form of autobiography, as it deals, not with the events, but with the thoughts of one's life, not with life's physical accidents of deed or circumstance, but with the spiritual moods and imaginative passions of the mind.

To know anything about oneself one must know all about others.

Duty is what one expects from others, it is not what one does oneself.

After a good dinner one can forgive anybody, even one's own relations.

Talk to every woman as if you loved her and to every man as if he bored you, and at the end of your first season you will have the reputation of possessing the most perfect social tact.

Man—poor, awkward, reliable, necessary man—belongs to a sex that has been rational for millions and millions of years. He can't help himself; it is in his race. The history of women is very different. They have always been picturesque protests against the mere existence of common-sense; they saw its dangers from the first.

More marriages are ruined nowadays by the common-sense of the husband than by anything else. How can a woman be expected to be happy with a man who insists on treating her as if she were a perfectly rational being.

It is very vulgar to talk about one's business. Only people like stock-brokers do that, and then merely at dinner-parties.

It is awfully hard work doing nothing. However, I don't mind hard work when there is no definite object of any kind.

To do nothing at all is the most difficult thing in the world, the most difficult and the most intellectual. To Plato, with his passion for wisdom, this was the noblest form of energy.

To Aristotle, with his passion for knowledge, this was the noblest form of energy also. It was to this that the passion for holiness led the saint and the mystic of mediæval days.

Youth! There is nothing like it. It is absurd to talk of the ignorance of youth. The only people to whose opinions I listen now with any respect are persons much younger than myself. They seem in front of me. Life has revealed to them her latest wonder.

Romance lives by repetition, and repetition converts an appetite into an art.

I adore simple pleasures. They are the last refuge of the complex.

There is nothing like youth. The middle-aged are mortgaged to life. The old are in life's lumber-room. But youth is the lord of life. Youth has a kingdom waiting for it. Everyone is born a king, and most people die in exile—like most kings.

All crime is vulgar, just as all vulgarity is crime.

Society, civilised society at least, is never very ready to believe anything to the detriment of those who are both rich and fascinating. It instinctively feels that manners are of more importance than morals, and in its opinion the highest respectability is of much less value than the possession of a good chef. And, after all, it is a very poor consolation to be told that the man who has given one a bad dinner or poor wine is irreproachable in his private life. Even the cardinal virtues cannot atone for half-cold entrees.

While, in the opinion of society, contemplation is the gravest thing of which any citizen can be guilty, in the opinion of the highest culture it is the proper occupation of man.

Life is terribly deficient in form. Its catastrophes happen in the wrong way and to the wrong people. There is a grotesque horror about its comedies, and its tragedies seem to culminate in farce. One is always wounded when one approaches it. Things last either too long or not long enough.

If a woman wants to hold a man she has merely to appeal to what is worst in him.

We are all in the gutter, but some of us are looking at the stars.

Beauty has as many meanings as man has moods. It is the symbol of symbols. It reveals everything, because it expresses nothing. When it shows us itself it shows us the whole fiery-coloured world.

Men always want to be a woman's first love. That is their clumsy vanity. Women have a more subtle instinct about things. What they like is to be a man's last romance.

Anything approaching to the free play of the mind is practically unknown amongst us. People cry out against the sinner, yet it is not the sinful but the stupid who are our shame. There is no sin except stupidity.

One regrets the loss even of one's worst habits. Perhaps one regrets them the most. They are such an essential part of one's personality.

It is through art, and through art only, that we can realise our perfection; through art and through art only, that we can shield ourselves from the sordid perils of actual existence.

A man who can dominate a London dinner-table can dominate the world. The future belongs to the dandy. It is the exquisites who are going to rule.

It often happens that the real tragedies of life occur in such an inartistic manner that they hurt us by their crude violence, their absolute incoherence, their absurd want of meaning, their entire lack of style. They affect us just as vulgarity affects us. They give us an impression of sheer brute force, and we revolt against that. Sometimes, however, a tragedy that possesses artistic elements of beauty crosses our lives. If these elements of beauty are real the whole thing simply appeals to our sense of dramatic effect. Suddenly we find that we are no longer the actors but the spectators of the play. Or rather we are both. We watch ourselves, and the mere wonder of the spectacle enthrals us.

When a woman finds out that her husband is absolutely indifferent to her, she either becomes dreadfully dowdy or wears very smart bonnets that some other woman's husband has to pay for.

It is immoral to use private property in order to alleviate the horrible evils that result from the institution of private property.

It is a mistake to think that the passion one feels in creation is ever really shown in the work one creates. Art is always more abstract than we fancy. Form and colour tell us of form and colour-that is all.

It is sometimes said that the tragedy of an artist's life is that he cannot realise his ideal. But the true tragedy that dogs the steps of most artists is that they realise their ideal too absolutely. For when the ideal is realised it is robbed of its wonder and its mystery, and becomes simply a new starting-point for an ideal that is other than itself.

People who go in for being consistent have just as many moods as others have. The only difference is that their moods are rather meaningless.

It is only shallow people who require years to get rid of an emotion. A man who is master of himself can end a sorrow as easily as he can invent a pleasure.

Good women have such a limited view of life, their horizon is so small, their interests so petty. The fact is they are not modern, and to be modern is the only thing worth being nowadays.

Discontent is the first step in the progress of a man or a nation.

Men marry because they are tired, women because they are curious. Both are disappointed.

All men are married women's property. That is the only true definition of what married women's property really is.

I am not in favour of this modern mania for turning bad people into good people at a moment's notice. As a man sows so let him reap.

Nothing refines but the intellect.

It is very painful for me to be forced to speak the truth. It is the first time in my life that I have ever been reduced to such a painful position, and I am really quite inexperienced in doing anything of the kind.

The man who regards his past is a man who deserves to have no future to look forward to.

Just as it is only by contact with the art of foreign nations that the art of a country gains that individual and separate life that we call nationality, so, by curious inversion, it is only by intensifying his own personality that the critic can interpret the personality of others; and the more strongly this personality enters into the interpretation the more real the interpretation becomes, the more satisfying, the more convincing, and the more true.

Man is least himself when he talks in his own person. Give him a mask, and he will tell you the truth.

All women become like their mothers: that is their tragedy. No man does: that is his.

Women are a fascinatingly wilful sex. Every woman is a rebel, and usually in wild revolt against herself.

One should always be in love. That is the reason one should never marry.

No man came across two ideal things. Few come across one.

To become the spectator of one's own life is to escape the suffering of life.

The state is to make what is useful. The individual is to make what is beautiful.

A community is infinitely more brutalised by the habitual employment of punishment than it is by the occasional occurrence of crime.

The systems that fail are those that rely on the permanency of human nature and not on its growth and development.

Jealousy, which is an extraordinary source of crime in modern life, is an emotion closely bound up with our conceptions of property, and under socialism and individualism will die out. It is remarkable that in communistic tribes jealousy is entirely unknown.

All art is immoral.

He to whom the present is the only thing that is present knows nothing of the age in which he lives. To realise the nineteenth century one must realise every century that has preceded it and that has contributed to its making.

Few parents nowadays pay any regard to what their children say to them. The old-fashioned respect for the young is fast dying out.

The history of woman is the history of the worst form of tyranny the world has ever known; the tyranny of the weak over the strong. It is the only tyranny that lasts.

The happiness of a married man depends on the people he has not married.

There is no one type for man. There are as many perfections as there are imperfect men. And while to the claims of charity a man may yield and yet be free, to the claims of conformity no man may yield and remain free at all.

A practical scheme is either a scheme that is already in existence or a scheme that could be carried out under existing conditions.

All imitation in morals and in life is wrong.

The world has been made by fools that wise men may live in it.

Women love us for our defects. If we have enough of them they will forgive us everything, even our gigantic intellects.

Society is a necessary thing. No man has any real success in this world unless he has got women to back him—and women rule society. If you have not got women on your side you are quite over. You might just as well be a barrister or a stockbroker or a journalist at once.

The worship of the senses has often, and with much justice, been decried; men feeling a natural instinct of terror about passions and sensations that seem stronger than themselves, and that they are conscious of sharing with the less highly organised forms of existence. But it is probable the true nature of the senses has never been understood, and that they have remained savage and animal merely because the world has sought to starve them into submission or to kill them by pain instead of aiming at making them elements of a new spirituality, of which a fine instinct for beauty will be the dominant characteristic.

Women appreciate cruelty more than anything else. They have wonderfully primitive instincts. We have emancipated them, but they remain slaves, looking for their master all the same. They love being dominated.

Those who try to lead the people can only do so by following the mob. It is through the voice of one crying in the wilderness that the way of the gods must be prepared.

Circumstances are the lashes laid on to us by life. Some of us have to receive them with bared ivory backs, and others are permitted to keep on a coat—that is the only difference.

Criticism is itself an art.... It is no more to be judged by any low standard of imitation or resemblance than is the work of poet or sculptor. The critic occupies the same relation to the work of art that he criticises as the artist does to the visible world of form and colour or the unseen world of passion and thought. He does not even require for the perfection of his art the finest materials. Anything will serve his purpose.

It is very much more difficult to talk about a thing than to do it. In the sphere of actual life that is, of course, obvious. Anybody can make history, only a great man can write it.

If we lived long enough to see the results of our actions it may be that those who call themselves good would be filled with a wild remorse and those whom the world calls evil stirred with a noble joy. Each little thing that we do passes into the great machine of life, which may grind our virtues to powder and make them worthless or transform our sins into elements of a new civilisation more marvellous and more splendid than any that has gone before.

Children begin by loving their parents; as they grow older they judge them, sometimes they forgive them.

We live in an age that reads too much to be wise and that thinks too much to be beautiful.

One should absorb the colour of life, but one should never remember its details. Details are always vulgar.

It will be a marvellous thing—the true personality of man—when we see it. It will grow naturally and simply flowerlike, or as a tree grows. It will not be at discord. It will never argue or dispute. It will not prove things. It will know everything, and yet it will not busy itself about knowledge. It will have wisdom. Its value will not be measured by material things. It will have nothing, and yet it will have everything, and whatever one takes from it it will still have, so rich it will be. It will not be always meddling with others or asking them to be like itself. It will love them because they will be different. And yet, while it will not meddle with others, it will help all, as a beautiful thing helps us, by being what it is. The personality of man will be very wonderful. It will be as wonderful as the personality of a child.

Cynicism is merely the art of seeing things as they are instead of as they ought to be.

Three addresses always inspire confidence, even in tradesmen.

If one doesn't talk about a thing it has never happened. It is simply expression that gives reality to things.

No man is able who is unable to get on, just as no woman is clever who can't succeed in obtaining that worst and most necessary of evils, a husband.

The one charm of the past is that it is the past. But women never know when the curtain has fallen. They always want a sixth act, and as soon as the interest of the play is entirely over they propose to continue it. If they were allowed their way every comedy would have a tragic ending and every tragedy would culminate in a farce. They are charmingly artificial, but they have no sense of art.

Each time that one loves is the only time that one has ever loved. Difference of object does not alter singleness of passion. It merely intensifies it.

The real tragedy of the poor is that they can afford nothing but self-denial. Beautiful sins, like beautiful things, are the privilege of the rich.

Human life is the one thing worth investigating. Compared to it there is nothing else of any value. It is true that as one watches life in its curious crucible of pain and pleasure one cannot wear over one's face a mask of glass nor keep the sulphurous fumes from troubling the brain and making the imagination turbid with monstrous fancies and misshapen dreams. There are poisons so subtle that to know their properties one has to sicken of them. There are maladies so strange that one has to pass through them if one seeks to understand their nature. And yet what a great reward one receives! How wonderful the whole world becomes to one! To note the curious, hard logic of passion and the emotional, coloured life of the intellect—to observe where they meet, and where they separate, at what point they are in unison and at what point they are in discord—there is a delight in that! What matter what the cost is? One can never pay too high a price for any sensation.

There is only one class in the community that thinks more about money than the rich, and that is the poor. The poor can think of nothing else. That is the misery of being poor.

To live is the rarest thing in the world. Most people exist—that is all.

Personality is a very mysterious thing. A man cannot always be estimated by what he does. He may keep the law, and yet be worthless. He may break the law, and yet be fine. He may be bad without ever doing anything bad. He may commit a sin against society, and yet realise through that sin his true perfection.

Mediæval art is charming, but mediæval emotions are out of date. One can use them in fiction, of course; but then the only things that one can use in fiction are the only things that one has ceased to use in fact.

Man is complete in himself.

What is a cynic? A man who knows the price of everything and the value of nothing.

It's the old, old story. Love—well, not at first sight—but love at the end of the season, which is so much more satisfactory.

No nice girl should ever waltz with such particularly younger sons! It looks so fast!

Good resolutions are useless attempts to interfere with scientific laws. Their origin is pure vanity. Their result is absolutely nil. They give us now and then some of those luxurious, sterile emotions that have a certain charm for the weak. That is all that can be said for them. They are simply cheques that men draw on a bank where they have no account.

What is the difference between literature and journalism? Journalism is unreadable and literature is unread.

I hope you have not been leading a double life, pretending to be wicked and being really good all the time. That would be hypocrisy.

My husband is a sort of promissory note; I am tired of meeting him.

Conscience makes egotists of us all.

Never trust a woman who wears mauve, whatever her age may be, or a woman over thirty-five who is fond of pink ribbons. It always means that they have a history.

There is a fatality about good resolutions-they are always made too late.

We can have in life but one great experience at best, and the secret of life is to reproduce that experience as often as possible.

Anybody can be good in the country. There are no temptations there. That is the reason why people who live out of town are so absolutely uncivilised. Civilisation is not by any means an easy thing to attain to. There are only two ways by which man can reach it. One is by being cultured, the other by being corrupt. Country people have no opportunity of being either, so they stagnate.

What nonsense people talk about happy marriages! A man can be happy with any woman so long as he does not love her.

The things one feels absolutely certain about are never true. That is the fatality of faith and the lesson of romance.

In the common world of fact the wicked are not punished nor the good rewarded. Success is given to the strong, failure thrust upon the weak.

Nothing should be able to harm a man except himself. Nothing should be able to rob a man at all. What a man really has is what is in him. What is outside of him should be a matter of no importance.

Modern morality consists in accepting the standard of one's age. I consider that for any man of culture to accept the standard of his age is a form of the grossest immorality.

Perplexity and mistrust fan affection into passion, and so bring about those beautiful tragedies that alone make life worth living. Women once felt this, while men did not, and so women once ruled the world.

Sin is a thing that writes itself across a man's, face. It cannot be concealed. People talk sometimes of secret vices. There are no such things.

If a wretched man has a vice it shows itself in the lines of his mouth, the drop of his eyelids, the moulding of his hands even.

There are sins whose fascination is more in the memory than in the doing of them, strange triumphs that gratify the pride more than the passions and give to the intellect a quickened sense of joy, greater than they bring or can ever bring to the senses.

No civilised man ever regrets a pleasure, and no uncivilised man ever knows what a pleasure is.

As for a spoiled life, no life is spoiled but one whose growth is arrested. If you want to mar a nature you have merely to reform it.

Socialism itself will be of value simply because it will lead to individualism.

Some years ago people went about the country saying that property has duties. It is perfectly true. Property not merely has duties, but has so many duties that its possession to any large extent is a bore. If property had simply pleasures we could stand it, but its duties make it unbearable.

It is through joy that the individualism of the future will develop itself. Christ made no attempt to reconstruct society, and consequently the individualism that He preached to man could be realised only through pain or in solitude.

Most people become bankrupt through having invested too heavily in the prose of life. To have ruined oneself over poetry is an honour.

The only artists I have ever known who are personally delightful are bad artists. Good artists exist simply on what they make, and consequently are perfectly uninteresting in what they are.

What are the virtues? Nature, Renan tells us, cares little about chastity, and it may be that it is to the shame of the Magdalen, and not to their own purity, that the Lucretias of modern life owe their freedom from stain. Charity, as even those of whose religion it makes a formal part have been compelled to acknowledge, creates a multitude of evils. The mere existence of conscience, that faculty of which people prate so much nowadays, and are so ignorantly proud, is a sign of our imperfect development. It must be merged in instinct before we become fine. Self-denial is simply a method by which man arrests his progress, and self-sacrifice a survival of the mutilation of the savage, part of that old worship of pain which is so terrible a factor in the history of the world, and which even now makes its victims day by day and has its altars in the land. Virtues! Who knows what the virtues are? Not you. Not I. Not anyone. It is well for our vanity that we slay the criminal, for if we suffered him to live he might show us what we had gained by his crime. It is well for his peace that the saint goes to his martyrdom. He is spared the sight of the horror of his harvest.

Nowadays all the married men live like bachelors and all the bachelors like married men.

The higher education of men is what I should like to see. Men need it so sadly.

The world is perfectly packed with good women. To know them is a middle-class education.

Hesitation of any kind is a sign of mental decay in the young, of physical weakness in the old.

Our husbands never appreciate anything in us. We have to go to others for that.

Most women in London nowadays seem to furnish their rooms with nothing but orchids, foreigners and French novels.

The canons of good society are, or should be, the same as the canons of art. Form is absolutely essential to it. It should have the dignity of a ceremony as well as its unreality, and should combine the insincere character of a romantic play with the wit and beauty that make such plays delightful to us. Is sincerity such a terrible thing? I think not. It is merely a method by which we can multiply our personalities.

The tragedy of old age is not that one is old but that one is young.

A great poet, a really great poet, is the most unpoetical of all creatures. But inferior poets are absolutely fascinating. The worse their rhymes are the more picturesque they look. The mere fact of having published a book of second-rate sonnets makes a man quite irresistible. He lives the poetry that he cannot write. The others write the poetry that they dare not realise.

Being adored is a nuisance. Women treat us just as humanity treats its gods. They worship us, and are always bothering us to do something for them.

If a man treats life artistically his brain is his heart.

The 'Peerage' is the one book a young man about town should know thoroughly, and it is the best thing in fiction the English have ever done.

The world has always laughed at its own tragedies, that being the only way in which it has been able to bear them. Consequently whatever the world has treated seriously belongs to the comedy side of things.

The only difference between the saint and the sinner is that every saint has a past and every sinner has a future.

What is termed sin is an essential element of progress. Without it the world would stagnate or grow old or becomes colourless. By its curiosity it increases the experience of the race. Through its intensified assertion of individualism it saves us from the commonplace. In its rejection of the current notions about morality it is one with the higher ethics.

Formerly we used to canonise our heroes. The modern method is to vulgarise them. Cheap editions of great books may be delightful, but cheap editions of great men are absolutely detestable.

Individualism does not come to man with any claims upon him at all. It comes naturally and inevitably out of man. It is the point to which all development tends. It is the differentiation to which all organisms grow. It is the perfection that is inherent in every mode of life and toward which every mode of life quickens. Individualism exercises no compulsion over man. On the contrary, it says to man that he should suffer no compulsion to be exercised over him. It does not try to force people to be good. It knows that people are good when they are let alone. Man will develop individualism out of himself. Man is now so developing individualism. To ask whether individualism is practical is like asking whether evolution is practical. Evolution is the law of life, and there is no evolution except towards individualism.

The longer I live the more keenly I feel that whatever was good enough for our fathers is not good enough for us. In art, as in politics, 'les grand pères ont toujours tort.'

No woman is a genius. Women are a decorative sex. They never have anything to say but they say it charmingly.

Humanity takes itself too seriously. It is the world's original sin. If the cave men had known how to laugh history would have been different.

I wonder who it was defined man as a rational animal. It was the most premature definition ever given. Man is many things, but he is not rational.

Thought and language are to the artist instruments of an art.

To get into the best society nowadays one has either to feed people, amuse people, or shock people—that is all.

You should never try to understand women. Women are pictures, men are problems. If you want to know what a woman really means—which, by the way, is always a dangerous thing to do—look at her, don't listen to her.

Ordinary women never appeal to one's imagination. They are limited to their century. No glamour ever transfigures them. One knows their minds as easily as one knows their bonnets. One can always find them. There is no mystery in any of them. They ride in the park in the morning and chatter at tea parties in the afternoon. They have their stereotyped smile and their fashionable mauve.

Don't run down dyed hair and painted faces. There is an extraordinary charm in them—sometimes.

To have been well brought up is a great drawback nowadays. It shuts one out from so much.

The people who have adored me—there have not been very many, but there have been some—have always insisted on living on long after I had ceased to care for them or they to care for me. They have become stout and tedious, and when I meet them they go in at once for reminiscences. That awful memory of women! What a fearful thing it is! And what an utter intellectual stagnation it reveals!

Examinations are pure humbug from beginning to end. If a man is a gentleman he knows quite enough, and if he is not a gentleman whatever he knows is bad for him.

Credit is the capital of a younger son, and he can live charmingly on it.

The object of art is not simply truth but complex beauty. Art itself is really a form of exaggeration, and selection, which is the very spirit of art, is nothing more than an intensified mode of over-emphasis.

The popular cry of our time is: 'Let us return to Life and Nature, they will recreate Art for us and send the red blood coursing through her veins; they will shoe her feet with swiftness and make her hand strong.' But, alas! we are mistaken in our amiable and well-meant efforts. Nature is always behind the age. And as for life, she is the solvent that breaks up Art, the enemy that lays waste her house.

There are only two kinds of women—the plain and the coloured. The plain women are very useful. If you want to gain a reputation for respectability you have merely to take them down to supper. The other women are very charming. They commit one mistake, however—they paint in order to try and look young.

The way of paradoxes is the way of truth. To test reality we must see it on the tight-rope. When the verities become acrobats we can judge them.

Life imitates art far more than art imitates life.... The Greeks with their quick, artistic instinct understood this, and set in the bride's chamber the statue of Hermes or of Apollo, that she might bear children as lovely as the works of art that she looked at in her rapture or her pain. They knew that life gains from art not merely spirituality, depth of thought and feeling, soul-turmoil or soul-peace, but that she can form herself on the very lines and colours of art, and can reproduce the dignity of Pheidias as well as the grace of Praxiteles. Hence came this objection to realism. They disliked it on purely social grounds. They felt that it inevitably makes people ugly, and they were perfectly right.

Faithfulness is to the emotional life what consistency is to the life of the intellect—simply a confession of failure.

There are many things that we would throw away if we were not afraid that others might pick them up.

What a fuss people make about fidelity! Why, even in love it is purely a question for physiology. It has nothing to do with our own will. Young men want to be faithful and are not; old men want to be faithless and cannot—that is all one can say.

Modernity of form and modernity of subject-matter are entirely and absolutely wrong. We have mistaken the common livery of the age for the vesture of the muses, and spent our days in the sordid streets and hideous suburbs of our vile cities when we should be out on the hillside with Apollo.

Certainly we are a degraded race, and have sold our birthright for a mess of facts.

Nothing can cure the soul but the senses, just as nothing can cure the senses but the soul.

I can stand brute force, but brute reason is quite unbearable. There is something unfair about its use. It is hitting below the intellect.

Those who live in marble or on painted panel know of life but a single exquisite instant, eternal, indeed, in its beauty but limited to one note of passion or one mood of calm. Those whom the poet makes live have their myriad emotions of joy and terror, of courage and despair, of pleasure and of suffering. The seasons come and go in glad or saddening pageant, and with winged or leaden feet the years pass by before them. They have their youth and their manhood, they are children, and they grow old. It is always dawn for St Helena as Veronese saw her at the window. Through the still morning air the angels bring her the symbol of God's pain. The cool breezes of the morning lift the gilt threads from her brow. On that little hill by the city of Florence, where the lovers of Giorgione are lying, it is always the solstice of noon—of noon made so languorous by summer suns that hardly can the slim, naked girl dip into the marble tank the round bubble of clear glass, and the long fingers of the lute player rest idly upon the chords. It is twilight always for the dancing nymphs whom Corot set free among the silver poplars of France. In eternal twilight they move, those frail, diaphanous figures, whose tremulous, white feet seem not to touch the dew-drenched grass they tread on. But those who walk in epos, drama, or romance see through the labouring months the young moons wax and wane, and watch the night from evening into morning star, and from sunrise into sun-setting can note the shifting day with all its gold and shadow. For them, as for us, the flowers bloom and wither, and the earth, that green-tressed goddess, as Coleridge calls her, alters her raiment for their pleasure. The statue is concentrated to one moment of perfection. The image stained upon the canvas possesses no spiritual element of growth or change. If they know nothing of death it is because they know little of life, for the secrets of life and death belong to those, and to those only, whom the sequence of time affects, and who possess not merely the present but the future, and can rise or fall from a past of glory or of shame. Movement, that problem of the visible arts, can be truly realised by literature alone. It is literature that shows us the body in its swiftness and the soul in its unrest.

Behind every exquisite thing that exists there is something tragic. Worlds have to be in travail that the merest flower may blow.

Beauty is a form of genius—is higher, indeed, than genius, as it needs no explanation. It is one of the great facts of the world, like sunlight, or springtime, or the reflection in dark water of that silver shell we call the moon. It cannot be questioned, it has its divine right of sovereignty.

The only way to get rid of a temptation is to yield to it. Resist it and your soul grows sick with longing for the things it has forbidden to itself.

Women spoil every romance by trying to make it last for ever.

He's sure to be a wonderful success. He thinks like a Tory and talks like a Radical, and that's so important nowadays.

Nowadays to be intelligible is to be found out.

We make gods of men and they leave us. Others make brutes of them and they fawn and are faithful.

The husbands of very beautiful women belong to the criminal classes.

To me beauty is the Wonder of wonders. It is only shallow people who do not judge by appearances.

The true mystery of the world is the visible, not the invisible.

The thoroughly well-informed man is the modern ideal. And the mind of the thoroughly well-informed man is a dreadful thing. It is like a bric-a-brac shop, all monsters and dust, with everything priced above its proper value.

Women have no appreciation of good looks in men—at least good women have none.

To influence a person is to give him one's own soul. He does not think his natural thoughts or burn with his natural passions. His virtues are not real to him. His sins, if there are such things as sins, are borrowed. He becomes an echo of someone else's music, an actor of a part that has not been written for him.

Those who are faithful know only the trivial side of love; it is the faithless who know love's tragedies.

An artist should create beautiful things, but should put nothing of his own life into them. We live in an age when men treat art as if it were meant to be a form of autobiography. We have lost the abstract sense of beauty.

A man cannot be too careful in the choice of his enemies. I have not got one who is a fool. They are all men of some intellectual power, and consequently they all appreciate me.

The value of an idea has nothing whatever to do with the sincerity of the man who expresses it.

I like persons better than principles, and I like persons with no principles better than anything else in the world.

He who would lead a Christ-like life is he who is perfectly and absolutely himself. He may be a great poet, or a great man of science; or a young student at the university, or one who watches sheep upon a moor; or a maker of dramas, like Shakespeare, or a thinker about God, like Spinoza; or a child who plays in a garden, or a fisherman who throws his nets into the sea. It does not matter what he is as long as he realises the perfection of the soul that is within him.

The aim of life is self-development. To realise one's nature perfectly—that is what each of us is here for.

There is no such thing as a good influence. All influence is immoral—immoral from the scientific point of view.

Words have not merely music as sweet as that of viol and lute, colour as rich and vivid as any that makes lovely for us the canvas of the Venetian or the Spaniard, and plastic form no less sure and certain than that which

48

reveals itself in marble or in bronze, but thought and passion and spirituality are theirs also—are theirs, indeed, alone.

There is nothing so absolutely pathetic as a really fine paradox. The pun is the clown among jokes, the well-turned paradox is the polished comedian, and the highest comedy verges upon tragedy, just as the keenest edge of tragedy is often tempered by a subtle humour. Our minds are shot with moods as a fabric is shot with colours, and our moods often seem inappropriate. Everything that is true is inappropriate.

The longer one studies life and literature the more strongly one feels that behind everything that is wonderful stands the individual, and that it is not the moment that makes the man but the man who creates the age.

To know the vintage and quality of a wine one need not drink the whole cask.

It is a sad thing to think of, but there is no doubt that genius lasts longer than beauty. That accounts for the fact that we all take such pains to over-educate ourselves.

The ugly and the stupid have the best of it in this world. They can sit at their ease and gape at the play. If they know nothing of victory they are at least spared the knowledge of defeat.

To have a capacity for a passion, and not to realise it is to make oneself incomplete and limited.

Even in actual life egotism is not without its attractions. When people talk to us about others they are usually dull. When they talk to us about themselves they are nearly always interesting, and if one could shut them up when they become wearisome as easily as one can shut up a book of which one has grown wearied they would be perfect absolutely.

Every great man nowadays has his disciples and it is invariably Judas who writes the biography.

Art finds her own perfection within, and not outside of, herself. She is not to be judged by any external standard of resemblance. She is a veil rather

49

than a mirror. She has flowers that no forest knows of, birds that no woodland possesses. She makes and unmakes many worlds, and can draw the moon from heaven with a scarlet thread. Hers are the 'forms more real than living man,' and hers the great archetypes, of which things that have existence are but unfinished copies. Nature has, in her eyes, no laws, no uniformity. She can work miracles at her will, and when she calls monsters from the deep they come. She can bid the almond-tree blossom in winter and send the snow upon the ripe cornfield. At her word the frost lays its silver finger on the burning mouth of June, and the winged lions creep out from the hollows of the Lydian hills. The dryads peer from the thicket as she passes by, and the brown fauns smile strangely at her when she comes near them. She has hawk-faced gods that worship her, and the centaurs gallop at her side.

In literature mere egotism is delightful.

If we live for aims we blunt our emotions. If we live for aims we live for one minute, for one day, for one year, instead of for every minute, every day, every year. The moods of one's life are life's beauties. To yield to all one's moods is to really live.

Many a young man starts in life with a natural gift for exaggeration which, if nurtured in congenial and sympathetic surroundings, or by the imitations of the best models, might grow into something really great and wonderful. But, as a rule, he comes to nothing. He either falls into careless habits of accuracy or takes to frequenting the society of the aged and the well-informed. Both things are equally fatal to his imagination.

The spirit of an age may be best expressed in the abstract ideal arts, for the spirit itself is abstract and ideal.

As for believing things, I can believe anything provided that it is quite incredible.

'Know thyself' was written over the portal of the antique world. Over the portal of the new world 'Be thyself' shall be written. And the message of Christ to man was simply: 'Be thyself.' That is the secret of Christ.

London is full of women who trust their husbands. One can always recognise them, they look so thoroughly unhappy.

For those who are not artists, and to whom there is no mode of life but the actual life of fact, pain is the only door to perfection.

The English public always feels perfectly at its ease when a mediocrity is talking to it.

Men always fall into the absurdity of endeavouring to develop the mind, to push it violently forward in this direction or in that. The mind should be receptive, a harp waiting to catch the winds, a pool ready to be ruffled, not a bustling busybody for ever trotting about on the pavement looking for a new bun shop.

There is nothing more beautiful than to forget, except, perhaps, to be forgotten.

All bad art comes from returning to life and nature, and elevating them into ideals. Life and nature may sometimes be used as part of art's rough material, but before they are of any real service to art they must be translated into artistic conventions. The moment art surrenders its imaginative medium it surrenders everything. As a method realism is a complete failure, and the two things that every artist should avoid are modernity of form and modernity of subject-matter.

Men may have women's minds just as women may have the minds of men.

London is too full of fogs and serious people. Whether the fogs produce the serious people or whether the serious people produce the fogs I don't know.

How marriage ruins a man! It's as demoralising as cigarettes, and far more expensive.

He must be quite respectable. One has never heard his name before in the whole course of one's life, which speaks volumes for a man nowadays.

Literature always anticipates life. It does not copy it, but moulds it to its purpose.

As long as a thing is useful or necessary to us or affects us in any way, either for pain or pleasure, or appeals strongly to our sympathies or is a vital part of the environment in which we live, it is outside the proper sphere of art.

I couldn't have a scene in this bonnet: it is far too fragile. A harsh word would ruin it.

Music creates for one a past of which one has been ignorant and fills one with a sense of sorrows that have been hidden from one's tears.

Nothing is so fatal to personality as deliberation.

I adore London dinner parties. The clever people never listen and the stupid people never talk.

Learned conversation is either the affection of the ignorant or the profession of the mentally unemployed.

The Academy is too large and too vulgar. Whenever I have gone there, there have been either so many people that I have not been able to see the pictures—which was dreadful, or so many pictures that I have not been able to see the people—which was worse.

All art is quite useless.

Beauty, real beauty, ends where an intellectual expression begins. Intellect is in itself a mode of exaggeration and destroys the harmony of any face. The moment one sits down to think one becomes all nose or all forehead or something horrid.

The one charm of marriage is that it makes a life of deception absolutely necessary for both parties.

Secrecy seems to be the one thing that can make modern life mysterious or marvellous to us. The commonest thing is delightful if one only hides it.

Conceit is one of the greatest of the virtues, yet how few people recognise it as a thing to aim at and to strive after. In conceit many a man and woman has found salvation, yet the average person goes on all-fours grovelling after modesty.

It is difficult not to be unjust to what one loves.

Humanity will always love Rousseau for having confessed his sins not to a friend but to the world.

Just as those who do not love Plato more than truth cannot pass beyond the threshold of the Academe, so those who do not love beauty more than truth never know the inmost shrine of art.

There is a fatality about all physical and intellectual distinction: the sort of fatality that seems to dog, through history, the faltering steps of kings. It is better not to be different from one's fellows.

To be born, or at any rate bred, in a handbag, whether it had handles or not, seems to me to display a contempt for the ordinary decencies of family life that reminds one of the worst excesses of the French Revolution.

Vice and virtue are to the artist materials for an art.

There must be a new Hedonism that shall recreate life and save it from that harsh, uncomely Puritanism that is having, in our own day, its curious revival. It must have its service of the intellect, certainly, yet it must never accept any theory or system that will involve the sacrifice of any mode of passionate experience. Its aim, indeed, is to be experience itself and not the fruits of experience, bitter or sweet as they may be. Of the æstheticism that deadens the senses, as of the vulgar profligacy that dulls them, it is to know nothing. But it is to teach man to concentrate himself upon the moments of a life that is itself but a moment.

Art never expresses anything but itself. It has an independent life, just as thought has, and develops purely on its own lines. It is not necessarily realistic in an age of realism nor spiritual in an age of faith. So far from being the creation of its time it is usually in direct opposition to it, and the only history that it preserves for us is the history of its own progress.

People who mean well always do badly. They are like the ladies who wear clothes that don't fit them in order to show their piety. Good intentions are invariably ungrammatical.

Man can believe the impossible, but man can never believe the improbable.

When art is more varied nature will, no doubt, be more varied also.

If a man is sufficiently imaginative to produce evidence in support of a lie he might just as well speak the truth at once.

The ancient historians gave us delightful fiction in the form of fact; the modern novelist presents us with dull facts under the guise of fiction.

Nature is no great mother who has home us. She is our own creation. It is in our brain that she quickens to life. Things are because we see them, and what we see and how we see it depends on the arts that have influenced us. To look at a thing is very different from seeing a thing. One does not see anything until one sees its beauty.

The proper school to learn art in is not life but art.

I won't tell you that the world matters nothing, or the world's voice, or the voice of society. They matter a good deal. They matter far too much.

I wouldn't marry a man with a future before him for anything under the sun.

I am the only person in the world I should like to know thoroughly, but I don't see any chance of it just at present.

Modern memoirs are generally written by people who have entirely lost their memories and have never done anything worth recording.

Education is an admirable thing, but it is well to remember from time to time that nothing that is worth knowing can be taught.

Women are like minors, they live upon their expectations.

Twisted minds are as natural to some people as twisted bodies.

It is the very passions about whose origin we deceive ourselves that tyrannise most strongly over us. Our weakest motives are those of whose nature we are conscious. It often happens that when we think we are experimenting on others we are really experimenting on ourselves.

Whenever a man does a thoroughly stupid thing it is always from the noblest motives.

I thought I had no heart. I find I have, and a heart doesn't suit me. Somehow it doesn't go with modern dress. It makes one look old, and it spoils one's career at critical moments.

I don't play accurately—anyone can play accurately—but I play with wonderful expression. As far as the piano is concerned sentiment is my forte. I keep science for life.

I delight in men over seventy. They always offer one the devotion of a lifetime.

Everybody who is incapable of learning has taken to teaching—that is really what our enthusiasm for education has come to.

Nature hates mind.

From the point of view of form the type of all the arts is the art of the musician. From the point of view of feeling the actor's craft is the type.

Where we differ from each other is purely in accidentals—in dress, manner, tone of voice, religious opinions, personal appearance, tricks of habit, and the like.

The more we study art the less we care for Nature. What art really reveals to us is Nature's lack of design, her curious crudities, her extraordinary monotony, her absolutely unfinished condition.... It is fortunate for us, however, that nature is so imperfect, as otherwise we should have had no art at all. Art is our spirited protest, our gallant attempt to teach Nature her proper place. As for the infinite variety of nature, that is a pure myth. It is not to be found in Nature herself. It resides in the imagination or fancy or cultivated blindness of the man who looks at her.

Facts are not merely finding a footing-place in history but they are usurping the domain of fancy and have invaded the kingdom of romance. Their chilling touch is over everything. They are vulgarising mankind.

Ordinary people wait till life discloses to them its secrets, but to the few, to the elect, the mysteries of life are revealed before the veil is drawn away. Sometimes this is the effect of art, and chiefly of the art of literature which deals immediately with the passions and the intellect. But now and then a complex personality takes the place and assumes the office of art, is, indeed, in its way a real work of art, Life having its elaborate masterpieces just as poetry has, or sculpture, or painting.

Thinking is the most unhealthy thing in the world, and people die of it just as they die of any other disease.

A cigarette is the perfect type of a perfect pleasure. It is exquisite and it leaves one unsatisfied.

The aim of the liar is simply to charm, to delight, to give pleasure. He is the very basis of civilised society.

It is quite a mistake to believe, as many people do, that the mind shows itself in the face. Vice may sometimes write itself in lines and changes of contour, but that is all. Our faces are really masks given to us to conceal our minds with.

What on earth should we men do going about with purity and innocence? A carefully thought-out buttonhole is much more effective.

The only difference between a caprice and a lifelong passion is that the caprice lasts a little longer.

People say sometimes that beauty is only superficial. That may be so, but at least it is not so superficial as thought is.

It is the spectator and not life that art really mirrors.

Nowadays people know the price of everything and the value of nothing.

Conscience and cowardice are really the same things. Conscience is the trade name of the firm—that is all.

In every sphere of life form is the beginning of things. The rhythmic, harmonious gestures of dancing convey, Plato tells us, both rhythm and harmony into the mind. Forms are the food of faith, cried Newman, in one of those great moments of sincerity that make us admire and know the man. He was right, though he may not have known how terribly right he was. The creeds are believed not because they are rational but because they are repeated. Yes; form is everything. It is the secret of life. Find expression for a sorrow and it will become dear to you. Find expression for a joy and you intensify its ecstasy. Do you wish to love? Use love's litany and the words will create the yearning from which the world fancies that they spring. Have you a grief that corrodes your heart? Learn its utterance from Prince Hamlet and Queen Constance and you will find that mere expression is a mode of consolation and that form, which is the birth of passion, is also the death of pain. And so, to return to the sphere of art, it is form that creates not merely the critical temperament but also the æsthetic instinct that reveals to one all things under the condition of beauty. Start with the worship of form and there is no secret in art that will not be revealed to you.

It is only the intellectually lost who ever argue.

Nowadays most people die of a sort of creeping common-sense, and discover when it is too late that the only things one never regrets are one's mistakes.

Lady Henry Wotton was a curious woman, whose dresses always looked as if they had been designed in a rage and put on in a tempest. She was usually in love with somebody, and, as her passion was never returned, she had kept all her illusions. She tried to look picturesque but only succeeded in being untidy.

Those who go beneath the surface do so at their peril.

With an evening coat and a white tie anybody, even a stockbroker, can gain a reputation for being civilised.

There is nothing so interesting as telling a good man or woman how bad one has been. It is intellectually fascinating. One of the greatest pleasures of having been wicked is that one has so much to say to the good.

Laws are made in order that people in authority may not remember them, just as marriages are made in order that the divorce court may not play about idly.

To get back one's youth one has merely to repeat one's follies.

Never marry a woman with straw-coloured hair. They are so sentimental.

The reason we all like to think so well of others is that we are all afraid for ourselves. The basis of optimism is sheer terror. We think that we are generous because we credit our neighbours with the possession of those virtues that are likely to be a benefit to us. We praise the banker that we may overdraw our account, and find good qualities in the high-wayman in the hope that he may spare our pockets. I have the greatest contempt for optimism.

Art begins with abstract decoration, with purely imaginative and pleasureable work dealing with what is unreal and non-existent. This is the first stage. Then life becomes fascinated with this new wonder, and asks to be admitted into the charmed circle. Art takes life as part of her rough material, recreates it and refashions it in fresh form; is absolutely indifferent to facts; invents, imagines, dreams, and keeps between herself and reality the impenetrable barrier of beautiful style, of decorative or ideal treatment. The third stage is when Life gets the upper hand and drives Art out into the wilderness. This is the true decadence, and it is from this that we are now suffering.

Good intentions have been the ruin of the world. The only people who have achieved anything have been those who have had no intentions at all.

I never take any notice of what common people say, and I never interfere with what charming people do.

You know I am not a champion of marriage. The real drawback to marriage is that it makes one unselfish, and unselfish people are colourless— they lack individuality. Still there are certain temperaments that marriage makes more complex. They retain their egotism, and add to it many other egos. They are forced to have more than one life. They become more highly organised, and to be highly organised is, I should fancy, the object of man's existence. Besides, every experience is of value, and whatever one may say against marriage it is certainly an experience.

Those who read the symbol do so at their peril.

I never talk during music—at least not during good music. If anyone hears bad music it is one's duty to drown it in conversation.

When critics disagree the artist is in accord with himself.

Faith is the most plural thing I know. We are all supposed to believe in the same thing in different ways. It is like eating out of the same dish with different coloured spoons.

Experience is of no ethical value. It is merely the name men give to their mistakes. Moralists have, as a rule, regarded it as a mode of warning, have claimed for it a certain ethical efficacy in the formation of character, have praised it as something that teaches us what to follow and shows us what to avoid. But there is no motive power in experience. It is as little of an active cause as conscience itself. All that it really demonstrates is that our future will be the same as our past and that the sin we have done once, and with loathing, we shall do many times, and with joy.

Sensations are the details that build up the stories of our lives.

No artist has ethical sympathies. An ethical sympathy in an artist is an unpardonable mannerism of style.

She looks like an 'edition de luxe' of a wicked French novel meant specially for the English market.

I never knew what terror was before; I know it now. It is as if a hand of ice were laid upon one's heart. It is as if one's heart were beating itself to death in some empty hollow.

We can forgive a man for making a useful thing as long as he does not admire it. The only excuse for making a useless thing is that one admires it intensely.

No artist desires to prove anything. Even things that are true can be proved.

One knows so well the popular idea of health. The English country gentleman galloping along after a fox—the unspeakable in pursuit of the uneatable.

People seldom tell the truths that are worth telling. We ought to choose our truths as carefully as we choose our lies and to select our virtues with as much thought as we bestow upon the selection of our enemies.

Soul and body, body and soul—how mysterious they are! There is animalism in the soul, and the body has its moments of spirituality. The senses can refine and the intellect can degrade. Who can say where the fleshly impulse ceases or the psychical impulse begins? How shallow are the arbitrary definitions of ordinary psychologists! And yet how difficult to decide between the claims of the various schools! Is the soul a shadow seated in the house of sin? Or is the body really in the soul, as Giordano Bruno thought? The separation of spirit from matter is a mystery, and the unison of spirit with matter is a mystery also.

Those who find beautiful meanings in beautiful things are the cultivated. For these there is hope.

There is no such thing as a moral or an immoral book. Books are well written or badly written-that is all.

Marriage is a sort of forcing house. It brings strange sins to fruit, and sometimes strange renunciations.

The moral life of man forms part of the subject-matter of the artist, but the morality of art consists in the perfect use of an imperfect medium.

A sense of duty is like some horrible disease. It destroys the tissues of the mind, as certain complaints destroy the tissues of the body. The catechism has a great deal to answer for.

They are the elect to whom beautiful things mean only beauty.

Those who find ugly meanings in beautiful things are corrupt without being charming. This is a fault.

Few people have sufficient strength to resist the preposterous claims of orthodoxy.

She wore far too much rouge last night and not quite enough clothes. That is always a sign of despair in a woman.

A virtue is like a city set upon a hill—it cannot be hid. We can conceal our vices if we care to—for a time at least—but a virtue will out.

Can't make out how you stand London society. The thing has gone to the dogs: a lot of damned nobodies talking about nothing.

You don't know what an existence they lead down there. It is pure, unadulterated country life. They get up early because they have so much to do, and go to bed early because they have so little to think about.

Nothing is so fatal to a personality as the keeping of promises, unless it be telling the truth.

Who cares whether Mr Ruskin's views on Turner are sound or not? What does it matter? That mighty and majestic prose of his, so fervid and so fiery coloured in its noble eloquence, so rich in its elaborate symphonic music, so sure and certain, at its best, in subtle choice of word and epithet, is, at least, as great a work of art as any of those wonderful sunsets that bleach or rot on their corrupted canvases in England's gallery—greater, indeed, one is apt to think at times, not merely because its equal beauty is more enduring but on account of the fuller variety of its appeal—soul speaking to soul in those long, cadenced lines, not through form and colour alone, though through these, indeed, completely and without loss, but with intellectual and emotional utterance, with lofty passion and with loftier thought, with imaginative insight and with poetic aim—greater, I always think, even as literature is the greater art.

Laughter is not at all a bad beginning for a friendship, and it is far the best ending for one.

Mrs Cheveley is one of those very modern women of our time who find a new scandal as becoming as a new bonnet, and air them both in the Park every afternoon at 5.30. I am sure she adores scandals, and that the sorrow of her life at present is that she can't manage to have enough of them.

The world divides actions into three classes: good actions, bad actions that you may do, and bad actions that you may not do. If you stick to the good actions you are respected by the good. If you stick to the bad actions that you may do you are respected by the bad. But if you perform the bad actions that no one may do then the good and the bad set upon you and you are lost indeed.

I choose my friends for their good looks, my acquaintances for their good characters, and my enemies for their good intellects.

The artist is the creator of beautiful things.

To me the word 'natural' means all that is middle class, all that is of the essence of Jingoism, all that is colourless and without form and void. It might be a beautiful word, but it is the most debased coin in the currency of language.

I pity any woman who is married to a man called John. She would probably never be allowed to know the entrancing pleasure of a single moment's solitude.

It is only when we have learned to love forgetfulness that we have learned the art of living.

To reveal art and conceal the artist is art's aim.

The world taken 'en masse' is a monster, crammed with prejudices, packed with prepossessions, cankered with what it calls virtues, a Puritan, a prig. And the art of life is the art of defiance. To defy—that is what we ought to live for, instead of living, as we do, to acquiesce.

Some resemblance the creative work of the critic will have to the work that has stirred him to creation, but it will be such resemblance as exists, not between nature and the mirror that the painter of landscape or figure may be supposed to hold up to her, but between nature and the work of the decorative artist. Just as on the flowerless carpets of Persia tulip and rose blossom indeed, and are lovely to look on, though they are not reproduced in visible shape or line; just as the pearl and purple of the sea shell is echoed in the church of St Mark at Venice; just as the vaulted ceiling of the wondrous chapel at Ravenna is made gorgeous by the gold and green and sapphire of the peacock's tail, though the birds of Juno fly not across it; so the critic reproduces the work that he criticises in a mode that is never imitative, and part of whose charm may really consist in the rejection of resemblance, and shows us in this way not merely the meaning but also the mystery of beauty, and by transforming each art into literature solves once for all the problem of art's unity.

Diversity of opinion about a work of art shows that the work is new, complex, and vital.

Nothing is more painful to me than to come across virtue in a person in whom I have never suspected its existence. It is like finding a needle in a bundle of hay. It pricks you. If we have virtue we should warn people of it.

The critic is he who can translate into another manner or a new material his impression of beautiful things.

Hopper is one of nature's gentlemen—the worst type of gentleman I know.

If one intends to be good one must take it up as a profession. It is quite the most engrossing one in the world.

I like Wagner's music better than anybody's. It is so loud that one can talk the whole time without other people hearing what one says.

All art is at once surface and symbol.

Childhood is one long career of innocent eavesdropping, of hearing what one ought not to hear.

The highest as the lowest form of criticism is a mode of autobiography.

The only things worth saying are those that we forget, just as the only things worth doing are those that the world is surprised at.

Maturity is one long career of saying what one ought not to say. That is the art of conversation.

Virtue is generally merely a form of deficiency, just as vice is an assertion of intellect.

People teach in order to conceal their ignorance, as people smile in order to conceal their tears.

To be unnatural is often to be great. To be natural is generally to be stupid.

To lie finely is an art, to tell the truth is to act according to nature.

People who talk sense are like people who break stones in the road: they cover one with dust and splinters.

Jesus said to man: You have a wonderful personality. Develop it. Be yourself. Don't imagine that your perfection lies in accumulating or possessing external things. Your perfection is inside of you. If only you could realise that you would not want to be rich. Ordinary riches can be stolen from a man, real riches cannot. In the treasury-house of your soul there are infinitely precious things that may not be taken from you. Try to so shape your life that external things will not harm you, and try also to get rid of personal property. It involves sordid preoccupation, endless industry, continual wrong. Personal property hinders individualism at every step.

When Jesus talks about the poor He simply means personalities, just as when He talks about the rich He simply means people who have not developed their personalities.

An echo is often more beautiful than the voice it repeats.

About Author

As a spokesman for aestheticism, he tried his hand at various literary activities: he published a book of poems, lectured in the United States and Canada on the new "English Renaissance in Art" and interior decoration, and then returned to London where he worked prolifically as a journalist. Known for his biting wit, flamboyant dress and glittering conversational skill, Wilde became one of the best-known personalities of his day. At the turn of the 1890s, he refined his ideas about the supremacy of art in a series of dialogues and essays, and incorporated themes of decadence, duplicity, and beauty into what would be his only novel, The Picture of Dorian Gray (1890). The opportunity to construct aesthetic details precisely, and combine them with larger social themes, drew Wilde to write drama. He wrote Salome (1891) in French while in Paris but it was refused a licence for England due to an absolute prohibition on the portrayal of Biblical subjects on the English stage. Unperturbed, Wilde produced four society comedies in the early 1890s, which made him one of the most successful playwrights of late-Victorian London.

At the height of his fame and success, while The Importance of Being Earnest (1895) was still being performed in London, Wilde had the Marquess of Queensberry prosecuted for criminal libel. The Marquess was the father of Wilde's lover, Lord Alfred Douglas. The libel trial unearthed evidence that caused Wilde to drop his charges and led to his own arrest and trial for gross indecency with men. After two more trials he was convicted and sentenced to two years' hard labour, the maximum penalty, and was jailed from 1895 to 1897. During his last year in prison, he wrote De Profundis (published posthumously in 1905), a long letter which discusses his spiritual journey through his trials, forming a dark counterpoint to his earlier philosophy of pleasure. On his release, he left immediately for France, never to return to Ireland or Britain. There he wrote his last work, The Ballad of Reading Gaol (1898), a long poem commemorating the harsh rhythms of prison life. He died destitute in Paris at the age of 46.

Early life

Oscar Wilde was born at 21 Westland Row, Dublin (now home of the Oscar Wilde Centre, Trinity College), the second of three children born to Sir William Wilde and Jane Wilde, two years behind William ("Willie"). Wilde's mother had distant Italian ancestry, and under the pseudonym "Speranza" (the Italian word for 'hope'), wrote poetry for the revolutionary Young Irelanders in 1848; she was a lifelong Irish nationalist. She read the Young Irelanders' poetry to Oscar and Willie, inculcating a love of these poets in her sons. Lady Wilde's interest in the neo-classical revival showed in the paintings and busts of ancient Greece and Rome in her home.

William Wilde was Ireland's leading oto-ophthalmologic (ear and eye) surgeon and was knighted in 1864 for his services as medical adviser and assistant commissioner to the censuses of Ireland. He also wrote books about Irish archaeology and peasant folklore. A renowned philanthropist, his dispensary for the care of the city's poor at the rear of Trinity College, Dublin, was the forerunner of the Dublin Eye and Ear Hospital, now located at Adelaide Road. On his father's side Wilde was descended from a Dutchman, Colonel de Wilde, who went to Ireland with King William of Orange's invading army in 1690. On his mother's side Wilde's ancestors included a bricklayer from County Durham who emigrated to Ireland sometime in the 1770s.

Wilde was baptised as an infant in St. Mark's Church, Dublin, the local Church of Ireland (Anglican) church. When the church was closed, the records were moved to the nearby St. Ann's Church, Dawson Street. Davis Coakley mentions a second baptism by a Catholic priest, Father Prideaux Fox, who befriended Oscar's mother circa 1859. According to Fox's own testimony in Donahoe's Magazine in 1905, Jane Wilde would visit his chapel in Glencree, County Wicklow, for Mass and would take her sons with her. She then asked Father Fox to baptise her sons. Fox described it in this way:

"I am not sure if she ever became a Catholic herself but it was not long before she asked me to instruct two of her children, one of them being the future erratic genius, Oscar Wilde. After a few weeks I baptized these two children, Lady Wilde herself being present on the occasion."

In addition to his children with his wife, Sir William Wilde was the father of three children born out of wedlock before his marriage: Henry Wilson, born in 1838, and Emily and Mary Wilde, born in 1847 and 1849, respectively, of different maternity to Henry. Sir William acknowledged paternity of his illegitimate children and provided for their education, but they were reared by his relatives rather than by his wife or with his legitimate children.

In 1855, the family moved to No. 1 Merrion Square, where Wilde's sister, Isola, was born in 1857. The Wildes' new home was larger and, with both his parents' sociality and success, it soon became a "unique medical and cultural milieu". Guests at their salon included Sheridan Le Fanu, Charles Lever, George Petrie, Isaac Butt, William Rowan Hamilton and Samuel Ferguson.

Until he was nine, Oscar Wilde was educated at home, where a French bonne and a German governess taught him their languages. He then attended Portora Royal School in Enniskillen, County Fermanagh from 1864 to 1871. Until his early twenties, Wilde summered at the villa, Moytura House, his father built in Cong, County Mayo. There the young Wilde and his brother Willie played with George Moore.

Isola died aged nine of meningitis. Wilde's poem "Requiescat" is written to her memory.

"Tread lightly, she is near

Under the snow

Speak gently, she can hear

the daisies grow"

University education: 1870s

Trinity College, Dublin

Wilde left Portora with a royal scholarship to read classics at Trinity College, Dublin, from 1871 to 1874, sharing rooms with his older brother Willie Wilde. Trinity, one of the leading classical schools, placed him with scholars such as R. Y. Tyrell, Arthur Palmer, Edward Dowden and his tutor, Professor J. P. Mahaffy who inspired his interest in Greek literature. As a student Wilde worked with Mahaffy on the latter's book Social Life in Greece. Wilde, despite later reservations, called Mahaffy "my first and best teacher" and "the scholar who showed me how to love Greek things". For his part, Mahaffy boasted of having created Wilde; later, he named him "the only blot on my tutorship".

The University Philosophical Society also provided an education, discussing intellectual and artistic subjects such as Rossetti and Swinburne weekly. Wilde quickly became an established member – the members' suggestion book for 1874 contains two pages of banter (sportingly) mocking Wilde's emergent aestheticism. He presented a paper titled "Aesthetic Morality". At Trinity, Wilde established himself as an outstanding student: he came first in his class in his first year, won a scholarship by competitive examination in his second, and then, in his finals, won the Berkeley Gold Medal, the University's highest academic award in Greek. He was encouraged to compete for a demyship to Magdalen College, Oxford – which he won easily, having already studied Greek for over nine years.

Magdalen College, Oxford

At Magdalen, he read Greats from 1874 to 1878, and from there he applied to join the Oxford Union, but failed to be elected.

Oscar Wilde posing for a photograph, looking at the camera. He is wearing a checked suit and a bowler hat. His right foot is resting on a knee high bench, and his right hand, holding gloves, is on it. The left hand is in the pocket.

Attracted by its dress, secrecy, and ritual, Wilde petitioned the Apollo Masonic Lodge at Oxford, and was soon raised to the "Sublime Degree of Master Mason". During a resurgent interest in Freemasonry in his third year, he commented he "would be awfully sorry to give it up if I secede from the

Protestant Heresy". Wilde's active involvement in Freemasonry lasted only for the time he spent at Oxford and his membership of the Apollo University Lodge lapsed after non-payment of subscriptions. He was deeply considering converting to Catholicism, discussing the possibility with clergy several times. In 1877, Wilde was left speechless after an audience with Pope Pius IX in Rome. He eagerly read Cardinal Newman's books, and became more serious in 1878, when he met the Reverend Sebastian Bowden, a priest in the Brompton Oratory who had received some high-profile converts. Neither his father, who threatened to cut off his funds, nor Mahaffy thought much of the plan; but mostly Wilde, the supreme individualist, balked at the last minute from pledging himself to any formal creed. On the appointed day of his baptism, Father Bowden received a bunch of altar lilies instead. Wilde retained a lifelong interest in Catholic theology and liturgy.

While at Magdalen College, Wilde became particularly well known for his role in the aesthetic and decadent movements. He wore his hair long, openly scorned "manly" sports though he occasionally boxed, and decorated his rooms with peacock feathers, lilies, sunflowers, blue china and other objets d'art, once remarking to friends whom he entertained lavishly, "I find it harder and harder every day to live up to my blue china." The line quickly became famous, accepted as a slogan by aesthetes but used against them by critics who sensed in it a terrible vacuousness. Some elements disdained the aesthetes, but their languishing attitudes and showy costumes became a recognised pose. Wilde was once physically attacked by a group of four fellow students, and dealt with them single-handedly, surprising critics. By his third year Wilde had truly begun to create himself and his myth, and saw his learning developing in much larger ways than merely the prescribed texts. This attitude resulted in his being rusticated for one term, when he nonchalantly returned to college late from a trip to Greece with Mahaffy.

Wilde did not meet Walter Pater until his third year, but had been enthralled by his Studies in the History of the Renaissance, published during Wilde's final year in Trinity. Pater argued that man's sensibility to beauty should be refined above all else, and that each moment should be felt to its fullest extent. Years later, in De Profundis, Wilde called Pater's Studies...

"that book that has had such a strange influence over my life". He learned tracts of the book by heart, and carried it with him on travels in later years. Pater gave Wilde his sense of almost flippant devotion to art, though it was John Ruskin who gave him a purpose for it. Ruskin despaired at the self-validating aestheticism of Pater, arguing that the importance of art lies in its potential for the betterment of society. Ruskin admired beauty, but believed it must be allied with, and applied to, moral good. When Wilde eagerly attended Ruskin's lecture series The Aesthetic and Mathematic Schools of Art in Florence, he learned about aesthetics as simply the non-mathematical elements of painting. Despite being given to neither early rising nor manual labour, Wilde volunteered for Ruskin's project to convert a swampy country lane into a smart road neatly edged with flowers.

Wilde won the 1878 Newdigate Prize for his poem "Ravenna", which reflected on his visit there the year before, and he duly read it at Encaenia. In November 1878, he graduated with a double first in his B.A. of Classical Moderations and Literae Humaniores (Greats). Wilde wrote to a friend, "The dons are 'astonied' beyond words – the Bad Boy doing so well in the end!"

Apprenticeship of an aesthete: 1880s

Debut in society

After graduation from Oxford, Wilde returned to Dublin, where he met again Florence Balcombe, a childhood sweetheart. She became engaged to Bram Stoker and they married in 1878. Wilde was disappointed but stoic: he wrote to her, remembering "the two sweet years – the sweetest years of all my youth" they had spent together. He also stated his intention to "return to England, probably for good." This he did in 1878, only briefly visiting Ireland twice.

Unsure of his next step, he wrote to various acquaintances enquiring about Classics positions at Oxford or Cambridge. The Rise of Historical Criticism was his submission for the Chancellor's Essay prize of 1879, which, though no longer a student, he was still eligible to enter. Its subject, "Historical Criticism among the Ancients" seemed ready-made for Wilde – with both his skill in composition and ancient learning – but he struggled to find his voice with the long, flat, scholarly style. Unusually, no prize was awarded that year. With the last of his inheritance from the sale of his father's houses, he set himself up as a bachelor in London. The 1881 British Census listed Wilde as a boarder at 1 (now 44) Tite Street, Chelsea, where Frank Miles, a society painter, was the head of the household. Wilde spent the next six years in London and Paris, and in the United States where he travelled to deliver lectures.

He had been publishing lyrics and poems in magazines since entering Trinity College, especially in Kottabos and the Dublin University Magazine. In mid-1881, at 27 years old, Poems collected, revised and expanded his poetic efforts. The book was generally well received, and sold out its first print run of 750 copies, prompting further printings in 1882. It was bound in a rich, enamel, parchment cover (embossed with gilt blossom) and printed on hand-made Dutch paper; Wilde presented many copies to the dignitaries and writers who received him over the next few years. The Oxford Union condemned the book for alleged plagiarism in a tight vote. The librarian, who had requested the book for the library, returned the presentation copy to Wilde with a note of apology. Richard Ellmann argues that Wilde's poem "Hélas!" was a sincere, though flamboyant, attempt to explain the dichotomies he saw in himself:

To drift with every passion till my soul

Is a stringed lute on which all winds can play

Punch was less enthusiastic, "The poet is Wilde, but his poetry's tame" was their verdict.

America: 1882

Aestheticism was sufficiently in vogue to be caricatured by Gilbert and Sullivan in Patience (1881). Richard D'Oyly Carte, an English impresario, invited Wilde to make a lecture tour of North America, simultaneously priming the pump for the US tour of Patience and selling this most charming aesthete to the American public. Wilde journeyed on the SS Arizona, arriving 2 January 1882, and disembarking the following day. Originally planned to last four months, it continued for almost a year due to the commercial success. Wilde sought to transpose the beauty he saw in art into daily life. This was a practical as well as philosophical project: in Oxford he had surrounded himself with blue china and lilies, and now one of his lectures was on interior design.

When asked to explain reports that he had paraded down Piccadilly in London carrying a lily, long hair flowing, Wilde replied, "It's not whether I did it or not that's important, but whether people believed I did it". Wilde believed that the artist should hold forth higher ideals, and that pleasure and beauty would replace utilitarian ethics.

Wilde and aestheticism were both mercilessly caricatured and criticised in the press; the Springfield Republican, for instance, commented on Wilde's behaviour during his visit to Boston to lecture on aestheticism, suggesting that Wilde's conduct was more a bid for notoriety rather than devotion to beauty and the aesthetic. T. W. Higginson, a cleric and abolitionist, wrote in "Unmanly Manhood" of his general concern that Wilde, "whose only distinction is that he has written a thin volume of very mediocre verse", would improperly influence the behaviour of men and women.

According to biographer Michèle Mendelssohn, Wilde was the subject of anti-Irish caricature and was portrayed as a monkey, a blackface performer and a Christy minstrel throughout his career. "Harper's Weekly put a sunflower-worshipping monkey dressed as Wilde on the front of the January 1882 issue. The magazine didn't let its reputation for quality impede its expression of what are now considered odious ethnic and racial ideologies. The drawing stimulated other American maligners and, in England, had a full page reprint in the Lady's Pictorial. ... When the National Republican discussed Wilde, it was to explain 'a few items as to the animal's pedigree.' And on 22 January 1882 the Washington Post illustrated the Wild Man of Borneo alongside Oscar Wilde of England and asked 'How far is it from this to this?' " Though his press reception was hostile, Wilde was well received in diverse settings across America; he drank whiskey with miners in Leadville, Colorado, and was fêted at the most fashionable salons in many cities he visited.

London life and marriage

74

His earnings, plus expected income from The Duchess of Padua, allowed him to move to Paris between February and mid-May 1883. While there he met Robert Sherard, whom he entertained constantly. "We are dining on the Duchess tonight", Wilde would declare before taking him to an expensive restaurant. In August he briefly returned to New York for the production of Vera, his first play, after it was turned down in London. He reportedly entertained the other passengers with "Ave Imperatrix!, A Poem on England", about the rise and fall of empires. E. C. Stedman, in Victorian Poets describes this "lyric to England" as "manly verse – a poetic and eloquent invocation". The play was initially well received by the audience, but when the critics wrote lukewarm reviews attendance fell sharply and the play closed a week after it had opened.

Wilde was left to return to England and lecturing on topics including Personal Impressions of America, The Value of Art in Modern Life, and Dress.

In London, he had been introduced in 1881 to Constance Lloyd, daughter of Horace Lloyd, a wealthy Queen's Counsel. She happened to be visiting Dublin in 1884, when Wilde was lecturing at the Gaiety Theatre. He proposed to her, and they married on 29 May 1884 at the Anglican St James's Church, Paddington in London. Constance's annual allowance of £250 was generous for a young woman (equivalent to about £25,600 in current value), but the Wildes had relatively luxurious tastes, and they had preached to others for so long on the subject of design that people expected their home to set new standards. No. 16, Tite Street was duly renovated in seven months at considerable expense. The couple had two sons, Cyril (1885) and Vyvyan (1886). Wilde became the sole literary signatory of George Bernard Shaw's petition for a pardon of the anarchists arrested (and later executed) after the Haymarket massacre in Chicago in 1886.

Robert Ross had read Wilde's poems before they met, and was unrestrained by the Victorian prohibition against homosexuality, even to the extent of estranging himself from his family. By Richard Ellmann's account, he was a precocious seventeen-year-old who "so young and yet so knowing, was determined to seduce Wilde". According to Daniel Mendelsohn, Wilde, who had long alluded to Greek love, was "initiated into homosexual sex" by Ross, while his "marriage had begun to unravel after his wife's second pregnancy, which left him physically repelled".

Prose writing: 1886–91

Journalism and editorship: 1886–89

Criticism over artistic matters in The Pall Mall Gazette provoked a letter in self-defence, and soon Wilde was a contributor to that and other journals during 1885–87. He enjoyed reviewing and journalism; the form suited his style. He could organise and share his views on art, literature and life, yet in a format less tedious than lecturing. Buoyed up, his reviews were largely chatty and positive. Wilde, like his parents before him, also supported the cause of Irish Nationalism. When Charles Stewart Parnell was falsely accused of inciting murder Wilde wrote a series of astute columns defending him in the Daily Chronicle.

His flair, having previously only been put into socialising, suited journalism and did not go unnoticed. With his youth nearly over, and a family to support, in mid-1887 Wilde became the editor of The Lady's World magazine, his name prominently appearing on the cover. He promptly renamed it The Woman's World and raised its tone, adding serious articles on parenting, culture, and politics, keeping discussions of fashion and arts. Two pieces of fiction were usually included, one to be read to children, the other for the ladies themselves. Wilde worked hard to solicit good contributions from his wide artistic acquaintance, including those of Lady Wilde and his wife Constance, while his own "Literary and Other Notes" were themselves popular and amusing.

The initial vigour and excitement he brought to the job began to fade as administration, commuting and office life became tedious. At the same time as Wilde's interest flagged, the publishers became concerned anew about circulation: sales, at the relatively high price of one shilling, remained low. Increasingly sending instructions to the magazine by letter, he began a new period of creative work and his own column appeared less regularly. In October 1889, Wilde had finally found his voice in prose and, at the end of the second volume, Wilde left The Woman's World. The magazine outlasted him by one issue.

If Wilde's period at the helm of the magazine was a mixed success from an organizational point of view, one can also argue that it played a pivotal role in his development as a writer and facilitated his ascent to fame. Whilst Wilde the journalist supplied articles under the guidance of his editors, Wilde the editor is forced to learn to manipulate the literary marketplace on his own terms.

Shorter fiction

Wilde published The Happy Prince and Other Tales in 1888, and had been regularly writing fairy stories for magazines. In 1891 he published two more collections, Lord Arthur Savile's Crime and Other Stories, and in September A House of Pomegranates was dedicated "To Constance Mary Wilde". "The Portrait of Mr. W. H.", which Wilde had begun in 1887, was first published in Blackwood's Edinburgh Magazine in July 1889. It is a short story, which reports a conversation, in which the theory that Shakespeare's sonnets were written out of the poet's love of the boy actor "Willie Hughes", is advanced, retracted, and then propounded again. The only evidence for this is two supposed puns within the sonnets themselves.

The anonymous narrator is at first sceptical, then believing, finally flirtatious with the reader: he concludes that "there is really a great deal to be said of the Willie Hughes theory of Shakespeare's sonnets." By the end fact and fiction have melded together. Arthur Ransome wrote that Wilde "read something of himself into Shakespeare's sonnets" and became fascinated with the "Willie Hughes theory" despite the lack of biographical evidence for the historical William Hughes' existence. Instead of writing a short but serious essay on the question, Wilde tossed the theory amongst the three characters of the story, allowing it to unfold as background to the plot. The story thus is an early masterpiece of Wilde's combining many elements that interested him: conversation, literature and the idea that to shed oneself of an idea one must first convince another of its truth. Ransome concludes that Wilde succeeds precisely because the literary criticism is unveiled with such a deft touch.

Though containing nothing but "special pleading", it would not, he says "be possible to build an airier castle in Spain than this of the imaginary William Hughes" we continue listening nonetheless to be charmed by the telling. "You must believe in Willie Hughes," Wilde told an acquaintance, "I almost do, myself."

Essays and dialogues

Wilde, having tired of journalism, had been busy setting out his aesthetic ideas more fully in a series of longer prose pieces which were published in the major literary-intellectual journals of the day. In January 1889, The Decay of Lying: A Dialogue appeared in The Nineteenth Century, and Pen, Pencil and Poison, a satirical biography of Thomas Griffiths Wainewright, in The Fortnightly Review, edited by Wilde's friend Frank Harris. Two of Wilde's four writings on aesthetics are dialogues: though Wilde had evolved professionally from lecturer to writer, he retained an oral tradition of sorts. Having always excelled as a wit and raconteur, he often composed by assembling phrases, bons mots and witticisms into a longer, cohesive work.

Wilde was concerned about the effect of moralising on art; he believed in art's redemptive, developmental powers: "Art is individualism, and individualism is a disturbing and disintegrating force. There lies its immense value. For what it seeks is to disturb monotony of type, slavery of custom, tyranny of habit, and the reduction of man to the level of a machine." In his only political text, The Soul of Man Under Socialism, he argued political conditions should establish this primacy – private property should be abolished, and cooperation should be substituted for competition. At the same time, he stressed that the government most amenable to artists was no government at all. Wilde envisioned a society where mechanisation has freed human effort from the burden of necessity, effort which can instead be expended on artistic creation. George Orwell summarised, "In effect, the world will be populated by artists, each striving after perfection in the way that seems best to him."

This point of view did not align him with the Fabians, intellectual socialists who advocated using state apparatus to change social conditions, nor did it endear him to the monied classes whom he had previously entertained.

78

Hesketh Pearson, introducing a collection of Wilde's essays in 1950, remarked how The Soul of Man Under Socialism had been an inspirational text for revolutionaries in Tsarist Russia but laments that in the Stalinist era "it is doubtful whether there are any uninspected places in which it could now be hidden".

Wilde considered including this pamphlet and The Portrait of Mr. W.H., his essay-story on Shakespeare's sonnets, in a new anthology in 1891, but eventually decided to limit it to purely aesthetic subjects. Intentions packaged revisions of four essays: The Decay of Lying, Pen, Pencil and Poison, The Truth of Masks (first published 1885), and The Critic as Artist in two parts. For Pearson the biographer, the essays and dialogues exhibit every aspect of Wilde's genius and character: wit, romancer, talker, lecturer, humanist and scholar and concludes that "no other productions of his have as varied an appeal". 1891 turned out to be Wilde's annus mirabilis; apart from his three collections he also produced his only novel.

The Picture of Dorian Gray

The first version of The Picture of Dorian Gray was published as the lead story in the July 1890 edition of Lippincott's Monthly Magazine, along with five others. The story begins with a man painting a picture of Gray. When Gray, who has a "face like ivory and rose leaves", sees his finished portrait, he breaks down. Distraught that his beauty will fade while the portrait stays beautiful, he inadvertently makes a Faustian bargain in which only the painted image grows old while he stays beautiful and young. For Wilde, the purpose of art would be to guide life as if beauty alone were its object. As Gray's portrait allows him to escape the corporeal ravages of his hedonism, Wilde sought to juxtapose the beauty he saw in art with daily life.

Reviewers immediately criticised the novel's decadence and homosexual allusions; The Daily Chronicle for example, called it "unclean", "poisonous", and "heavy with the mephitic odours of moral and spiritual putrefaction". Wilde vigorously responded, writing to the editor of the Scots Observer, in which he clarified his stance on ethics and aesthetics in art – "If a work of art is rich and vital and complete, those who have artistic instincts will see its beauty and those to whom ethics appeal more strongly will see its moral lesson." He nevertheless revised it extensively for book publication in 1891: six new chapters were added, some overtly decadent passages and homo-eroticism excised, and a preface was included consisting of twenty two epigrams, such as "Books are well written, or badly written. That is all."

Contemporary reviewers and modern critics have postulated numerous possible sources of the story, a search Jershua McCormack argues is futile because Wilde "has tapped a root of Western folklore so deep and ubiquitous that the story has escaped its origins and returned to the oral tradition." Wilde claimed the plot was "an idea that is as old as the history of literature but to which I have given a new form". Modern critic Robin McKie considered the novel to be technically mediocre, saying that the conceit of the plot had guaranteed its fame, but the device is never pushed to its full.

Theatrical career: 1892–95

Salomé

The 1891 census records the Wildes' residence at 16 Tite Street, where he lived with his wife Constance and two sons. Wilde though, not content with being better known than ever in London, returned to Paris in October 1891, this time as a respected writer. He was received at the salons littéraires, including the famous mardis of Stéphane Mallarmé, a renowned symbolist poet of the time. Wilde's two plays during the 1880s, Vera; or, The Nihilists and The Duchess of Padua, had not met with much success. He had continued his interest in the theatre and now, after finding his voice in prose, his thoughts turned again to the dramatic form as the biblical iconography of Salome filled his mind. One evening, after discussing depictions of Salome throughout history, he returned to his hotel and noticed a blank copybook lying on the desk, and it occurred to him to write in it what he had been saying. The result was a new play, Salomé, written rapidly and in French.

A tragedy, it tells the story of Salome, the stepdaughter of the tetrarch Herod Antipas, who, to her stepfather's dismay but mother's delight, requests the head of Jokanaan (John the Baptist) on a silver platter as a reward for dancing the Dance of the Seven Veils. When Wilde returned to London just

80

before Christmas the Paris Echo referred to him as "le great event" of the season. Rehearsals of the play, starring Sarah Bernhardt, began but the play was refused a licence by the Lord Chamberlain, since it depicted biblical characters. Salome was published jointly in Paris and London in 1893, but was not performed until 1896 in Paris, during Wilde's later incarceration.

Comedies of society

Wilde, who had first set out to irritate Victorian society with his dress and talking points, then outrage it with Dorian Gray, his novel of vice hidden beneath art, finally found a way to critique society on its own terms. Lady Windermere's Fan was first performed on 20 February 1892 at St James's Theatre, packed with the cream of society. On the surface a witty comedy, there is subtle subversion underneath: "it concludes with collusive concealment rather than collective disclosure". The audience, like Lady Windermere, are forced to soften harsh social codes in favour of a more nuanced view. The play was enormously popular, touring the country for months, but largely trashed by conservative critics. It was followed by A Woman of No Importance in 1893, another Victorian comedy, revolving around the spectre of illegitimate births, mistaken identities and late revelations. Wilde was commissioned to write two more plays and An Ideal Husband, written in 1894, followed in January 1895.

Peter Raby said these essentially English plays were well-pitched, "Wilde, with one eye on the dramatic genius of Ibsen, and the other on the commercial competition in London's West End, targeted his audience with adroit precision".

Queensberry family

In mid-1891 Lionel Johnson introduced Wilde to Lord Alfred Douglas, Johnson's cousin and an undergraduate at Oxford at the time. Known to his family and friends as "Bosie", he was a handsome and spoilt young man. An intimate friendship sprang up between Wilde and Douglas and by 1893 Wilde was infatuated with Douglas and they consorted together regularly in a tempestuous affair. If Wilde was relatively indiscreet, even flamboyant, in the way he acted, Douglas was reckless in public. Wilde, who was earning up to

£100 a week from his plays (his salary at The Woman's World had been £6), indulged Douglas's every whim: material, artistic or sexual.

Douglas soon initiated Wilde into the Victorian underground of gay prostitution and Wilde was introduced to a series of young working-class male prostitutes from 1892 onwards by Alfred Taylor. These infrequent rendezvous usually took the same form: Wilde would meet the boy, offer him gifts, dine him privately and then take him to a hotel room. Unlike Wilde's idealised, pederastic relations with Ross, John Gray, and Douglas, all of whom remained part of his aesthetic circle, these consorts were uneducated and knew nothing of literature. Soon his public and private lives had become sharply divided; in De Profundis he wrote to Douglas that "It was like feasting with panthers; the danger was half the excitement... I did not know that when they were to strike at me it was to be at another's piping and at another's pay."

Douglas and some Oxford friends founded a journal, The Chameleon, to which Wilde "sent a page of paradoxes originally destined for the Saturday Review". "Phrases and Philosophies for the Use of the Young" was to come under attack six months later at Wilde's trial, where he was forced to defend the magazine to which he had sent his work. In any case, it became unique: The Chameleon was not published again.

Lord Alfred's father, the Marquess of Queensberry, was known for his outspoken atheism, brutish manner and creation of the modern rules of boxing. Queensberry, who feuded regularly with his son, confronted Wilde and Lord Alfred about the nature of their relationship several times, but Wilde was able to mollify him. In June 1894, he called on Wilde at 16 Tite Street, without an appointment, and clarified his stance: "I do not say that you are it, but you look it, and pose at it, which is just as bad. And if I catch you and my son again in any public restaurant I will thrash you" to which Wilde responded: "I don't know what the Queensberry rules are, but the Oscar Wilde rule is to shoot on sight". His account in De Profundis was less triumphant: "It was when, in my library at Tite Street, waving his small hands in the air in epileptic fury, your father... stood uttering every foul word his foul mind could think of, and screaming the loathsome threats he afterwards with such cunning carried out". Queensberry only described the scene once, saying Wilde had "shown him the white feather", meaning he had acted in a cowardly way. Though trying to remain calm, Wilde saw that he was becoming ensnared in a brutal family quarrel. He did not wish to bear Queensberry's insults, but he knew to confront him could lead to disaster were his liaisons disclosed publicly.

The Importance of Being Earnest

Wilde's final play again returns to the theme of switched identities: the play's two protagonists engage in "bunburying" (the maintenance of alternative personas in the town and country) which allows them to escape Victorian social mores. Earnest is even lighter in tone than Wilde's earlier comedies. While their characters often rise to serious themes in moments of crisis, Earnest lacks the by-now stock Wildean characters: there is no "woman with a past", the principals are neither villainous nor cunning, simply idle cultivés, and the idealistic young women are not that innocent. Mostly set in drawing rooms and almost completely lacking in action or violence, Earnest lacks the self-conscious decadence found in The Picture of Dorian Gray and Salome.

The play, now considered Wilde's masterpiece, was rapidly written in Wilde's artistic maturity in late 1894. It was first performed on 14 February 1895, at St James's Theatre in London, Wilde's second collaboration with George Alexander, the actor-manager. Both author and producer assiduously revised, prepared and rehearsed every line, scene and setting in the months before the premiere, creating a carefully constructed representation of late-Victorian society, yet simultaneously mocking it. During rehearsal Alexander requested that Wilde shorten the play from four acts to three, which the author did. Premieres at St James's seemed like "brilliant parties", and the opening of The Importance of Being Earnest was no exception. Allan Aynesworth (who played Algernon) recalled to Hesketh Pearson, "In my fifty-three years of acting, I never remember a greater triumph than [that] first night." Earnest's immediate reception as Wilde's best work to date finally crystallised his fame into a solid artistic reputation. The Importance of Being Earnest remains his most popular play.

Wilde's professional success was mirrored by an escalation in his feud with Queensberry. Queensberry had planned to insult Wilde publicly by throwing a bouquet of rotting vegetables onto the stage; Wilde was tipped off and had Queensberry barred from entering the theatre. Fifteen weeks later Wilde was in prison.

Trials

Wilde v. Queensberry

On 18 February 1895, the Marquess left his calling card at Wilde's club, the Albemarle, inscribed: "For Oscar Wilde, posing somdomite" . Wilde, encouraged by Douglas and against the advice of his friends, initiated a private prosecution against Queensberry for libel, since the note amounted to a public accusation that Wilde had committed the crime of sodomy.

Queensberry was arrested for criminal libel; a charge carrying a possible sentence of up to two years in prison. Under the 1843 Libel Act, Queensberry could avoid conviction for libel only by demonstrating that his accusation was in fact true, and furthermore that there was some "public benefit" to having made the accusation openly. Queensberry's lawyers thus hired private detectives to find evidence of Wilde's homosexual liaisons.

Wilde's friends had advised him against the prosecution at a Saturday Review meeting at the Café Royal on 24 March 1895; Frank Harris warned him that "they are going to prove sodomy against you" and advised him to flee to France. Wilde and Douglas walked out in a huff, Wilde saying "it is at such moments as these that one sees who are one's true friends". The scene was witnessed by George Bernard Shaw who recalled it to Arthur Ransome a day or so before Ransome's trial for libelling Douglas in 1913. To Ransome it confirmed what he had said in his 1912 book on Wilde; that Douglas's rivalry for Wilde with Robbie Ross and his arguments with his father had resulted in Wilde's public disaster; as Wilde wrote in De Profundis. Douglas lost his case. Shaw included an account of the argument between Harris, Douglas and Wilde in the preface to his play The Dark Lady of the Sonnets.

The libel trial became a cause célèbre as salacious details of Wilde's private life with Taylor and Douglas began to appear in the press. A team of private detectives had directed Queensberry's lawyers, led by Edward Carson QC, to the world of the Victorian underground. Wilde's association with blackmailers and male prostitutes, cross-dressers and homosexual brothels was recorded, and various persons involved were interviewed, some being coerced to appear as witnesses since they too were accomplices to the crimes of which Wilde was accused.

The trial opened on 3 April 1895 amid scenes of near hysteria both in the press and the public galleries. The extent of the evidence massed against Wilde forced him to declare meekly, "I am the prosecutor in this case". Wilde's lawyer, Sir Edward George Clarke, opened the case by pre-emptively asking Wilde about two suggestive letters Wilde had written to Douglas, which the defence had in its possession. He characterised the first as a "prose sonnet" and admitted that the "poetical language" might seem strange to the court but claimed its intent was innocent. Wilde stated that the letters had been obtained by blackmailers who had attempted to extort money from him, but he had refused, suggesting they should take the £60 (equal to £6,800 today) offered, "unusual for a prose piece of that length". He claimed to regard the letters as works of art rather than something of which to be ashamed.

Carson, a fellow Dubliner who had attended Trinity College, Dublin at the same time as Wilde, cross-examined Wilde on how he perceived the moral content of his works. Wilde replied with characteristic wit and flippancy, claiming that works of art are not capable of being moral or immoral but only well or poorly made, and that only "brutes and illiterates", whose views on art "are incalculably stupid", would make such judgements about art. Carson, a leading barrister, diverged from the normal practice of asking closed questions. Carson pressed Wilde on each topic from every angle, squeezing out nuances of meaning from Wilde's answers, removing them from their aesthetic context and portraying Wilde as evasive and decadent. While Wilde won the most laughs from the court, Carson scored the most legal points. To undermine Wilde's credibility, and to justify Queensberry's description of Wilde as a "posing somdomite", Carson drew from the witness an admission of his capacity for "posing", by demonstrating that he had lied about his age on oath. Playing on this, he returned to the topic throughout his cross-examination. Carson also tried to justify Queensberry's characterization by quoting from Wilde's novel, The Picture of Dorian Gray, referring in particular to a scene in the second chapter, in which Lord Henry Wotton explains his decadent philosophy to Dorian, an "innocent young man", in Carson's words.

Carson then moved to the factual evidence and questioned Wilde about his friendships with younger, lower-class men. Wilde admitted being on a first-name basis and lavishing gifts upon them, but insisted that nothing untoward had occurred and that the men were merely good friends of his. Carson repeatedly pointed out the unusual nature of these relationships and insinuated that the men were prostitutes. Wilde replied that he did not believe in social barriers, and simply enjoyed the society of young men. Then Carson asked Wilde directly whether he had ever kissed a certain servant boy, Wilde responded, "Oh, dear no. He was a particularly plain boy – unfortunately ugly – I pitied him for it." Carson pressed him on the answer, repeatedly asking why the boy's ugliness was relevant. Wilde hesitated, then for the first time became flustered: "You sting me and insult me and try to unnerve me; and at times one says things flippantly when one ought to speak more seriously."

In his opening speech for the defence, Carson announced that he had located several male prostitutes who were to testify that they had had sex with Wilde. On the advice of his lawyers, Wilde dropped the prosecution. Queensberry was found not guilty, as the court declared that his accusation that Wilde was "posing as a Somdomite " was justified, "true in substance and in fact". Under the Libel Act 1843, Queensberry's acquittal rendered Wilde legally liable for the considerable expenses Queensberry had incurred in his defence, which left Wilde bankrupt.

Regina v. Wilde

After Wilde left the court, a warrant for his arrest was applied for on charges of sodomy and gross indecency. Robbie Ross found Wilde at the Cadogan Hotel, Pont Street, Knightsbridge, with Reginald Turner; both men advised Wilde to go at once to Dover and try to get a boat to France; his mother advised him to stay and fight. Wilde, lapsing into inaction, could only say, "The train has gone. It's too late." On 6 April 1895, Wilde was arrested for "gross indecency" under Section 11 of the Criminal Law Amendment Act 1885, a term meaning homosexual acts not amounting to buggery (an offence under a separate statute). At Wilde's instruction, Ross and Wilde's butler forced their way into the bedroom and library of 16 Tite Street, packing some personal effects, manuscripts, and letters. Wilde was then imprisoned on remand at Holloway where he received daily visits from Douglas.

Events moved quickly and his prosecution opened on 26 April 1895, before Mr Justice Charles. Wilde pleaded not guilty. He had already begged Douglas to leave London for Paris, but Douglas complained bitterly, even wanting to give evidence; he was pressed to go and soon fled to the Hotel du Monde. Fearing persecution, Ross and many others also left the United Kingdom during this time. Under cross examination Wilde was at first hesitant, then spoke eloquently:

Charles Gill (prosecuting): What is "the love that dare not speak its name"?

Wilde: "The love that dare not speak its name" in this century is such a great affection of an elder for a younger man as there was between David and Jonathan, such as Plato made the very basis of his philosophy, and such as you find in the sonnets of Michelangelo and Shakespeare. It is that deep spiritual affection that is as pure as it is perfect. It dictates and pervades great works of art, like those of Shakespeare and Michelangelo, and those two letters of mine, such as they are. It is in this century misunderstood, so much misunderstood that it may be described as "the love that dare not speak its name", and on that account of it I am placed where I am now. It is beautiful, it is fine, it is the noblest form of affection. There is nothing unnatural about it. It is intellectual, and it repeatedly exists between an older and a younger man, when the older man has intellect, and the younger man has all the joy, hope and glamour of life before him. That it should be so, the world does not understand. The world mocks at it, and sometimes puts one in the pillory for it.

This response was counter-productive in a legal sense as it only served to reinforce the charges of homosexual behaviour.

The trial ended with the jury unable to reach a verdict. Wilde's counsel, Sir Edward Clarke, was finally able to get a magistrate to allow Wilde and his friends to post bail. The Reverend Stewart Headlam put up most of the £5,000 surety required by the court, having disagreed with Wilde's treatment by the press and the courts. Wilde was freed from Holloway and, shunning attention, went into hiding at the house of Ernest and Ada Leverson, two of his firm friends. Edward Carson approached Frank Lockwood QC, the Solicitor General and asked "Can we not let up on the fellow now?" Lockwood answered that he would like to do so, but feared that the case had become too politicised to be dropped.

The final trial was presided over by Mr Justice Wills. On 25 May 1895 Wilde and Alfred Taylor were convicted of gross indecency and sentenced to two years' hard labour. The judge described the sentence, the maximum allowed, as "totally inadequate for a case such as this", and that the case was "the worst case I have ever tried". Wilde's response "And I? May I say nothing, my Lord?" was drowned out in cries of "Shame" in the courtroom.

Imprisonment

When first I was put into prison some people advised me to try and forget who I was. It was ruinous advice. It is only by realising what I am that I have found comfort of any kind. Now I am advised by others to try on my release to forget that I have ever been in a prison at all. I know that would be equally fatal. It would mean that I would always be haunted by an intolerable sense of disgrace, and that those things that are meant for me as much as for anybody else – the beauty of the sun and moon, the pageant of the seasons, the music of daybreak and the silence of great nights, the rain falling through the leaves, or the dew creeping over the grass and making it silver – would all be tainted for me, and lose their healing power, and their power of communicating joy. To regret one's own experiences is to arrest one's own development. To deny one's own experiences is to put a lie into the lips of one's own life. It is no less than a denial of the soul.

De Profundis

Wilde was incarcerated from 25 May 1895 to 18 May 1897.

He first entered Newgate Prison in London for processing, then was moved to Pentonville Prison, where the "hard labour" to which he had been sentenced consisted of many hours of walking a treadmill and picking oakum (separating the fibres in scraps of old navy ropes), and where prisoners were allowed to read only the Bible and The Pilgrim's Progress.

A few months later he was moved to Wandsworth Prison in London. Inmates there also followed the regimen of "hard labour, hard fare and a hard bed", which wore harshly on Wilde's delicate health. In November he collapsed during chapel from illness and hunger. His right ear drum was ruptured in the fall, an injury that later contributed to his death. He spent two months in the infirmary.

Richard B. Haldane, the Liberal MP and reformer, visited Wilde and had him transferred in November to Reading Gaol, 30 miles (48 km) west of London on 23 November 1895. The transfer itself was the lowest point of his incarceration, as a crowd jeered and spat at him on the railway platform. He spent the remainder of his sentence there, addressed and identified only as "C33" – the occupant of the third cell on the third floor of C ward.

About five months after Wilde arrived at Reading Gaol, Charles Thomas Wooldridge, a trooper in the Royal Horse Guards, was brought to Reading to await his trial for murdering his wife on 29 March 1896; on 17 June Wooldridge was sentenced to death and returned to Reading for his execution, which took place on Tuesday, 7 July 1896 – the first hanging at Reading in 18 years. From Wooldridge's hanging, Wilde later wrote The Ballad of Reading Gaol.

Wilde was not, at first, even allowed paper and pen but Haldane eventually succeeded in allowing access to books and writing materials. Wilde requested, among others: the Bible in French; Italian and German grammars; some Ancient Greek texts, Dante's Divine Comedy, Joris-Karl Huysmans's new French novel about Christian redemption En route, and essays by St Augustine, Cardinal Newman and Walter Pater.

Between January and March 1897 Wilde wrote a 50,000-word letter to Douglas. He was not allowed to send it, but was permitted to take it with him when released from prison. In reflective mode, Wilde coldly examines his career to date, how he had been a colourful agent provocateur in Victorian society, his art, like his paradoxes, seeking to subvert as well as sparkle. His own estimation of himself was: one who "stood in symbolic relations to the art and culture of my age". It was from these heights that his life with Douglas began, and Wilde examines that particularly closely, repudiating him for what Wilde finally sees as his arrogance and vanity: he had not forgotten Douglas' remark, when he was ill, "When you are not on your pedestal you are not interesting." Wilde blamed himself, though, for the ethical degradation of character that he allowed Douglas to bring about in him and took responsibility for his own fall, "I am here for having tried to put your father in prison." The first half concludes with Wilde forgiving Douglas, for his own sake as much as Douglas's. The second half of the letter traces Wilde's spiritual journey of redemption and fulfilment through his prison reading. He realised that his ordeal had filled his soul with the fruit of experience, however bitter it tasted at the time.

... I wanted to eat of the fruit of all the trees in the garden of the world ... And so, indeed, I went out, and so I lived. My only mistake was that I confined myself so exclusively to the trees of what seemed to me the sun-lit side of the garden, and shunned the other side for its shadow and its gloom.

Wilde was released from prison on 19 May 1897 and sailed that evening for Dieppe, France. He never returned to the UK.

On his release, he gave the manuscript to Ross, who may or may not have carried out Wilde's instructions to send a copy to Douglas (who later denied having received it). The letter was partially published in 1905 as De Profundis; its complete and correct publication first occurred in 1962 in The Letters of Oscar Wilde.

Decline: 1897–1900

Exile

Though Wilde's health had suffered greatly from the harshness and diet of prison, he had a feeling of spiritual renewal. He immediately wrote to the

Society of Jesus requesting a six-month Catholic retreat; when the request was denied, Wilde wept. "I intend to be received into the Catholic Church before long", Wilde told a journalist who asked about his religious intentions.

He spent his last three years impoverished and in exile. He took the name "Sebastian Melmoth", after Saint Sebastian and the titular character of Melmoth the Wanderer (a Gothic novel by Charles Maturin, Wilde's great-uncle). Wilde wrote two long letters to the editor of the Daily Chronicle, describing the brutal conditions of English prisons and advocating penal reform. His discussion of the dismissal of Warder Martin for giving biscuits to an anaemic child prisoner, repeated the themes of the corruption and degeneration of punishment that he had earlier outlined in The Soul of Man under Socialism.

Wilde spent mid-1897 with Robert Ross in the seaside village of Berneval-le-Grand in northern France, where he wrote The Ballad of Reading Gaol, narrating the execution of Charles Thomas Wooldridge, who murdered his wife in a rage at her infidelity. It moves from an objective story-telling to symbolic identification with the prisoners. No attempt is made to assess the justice of the laws which convicted them but rather the poem highlights the brutalisation of the punishment that all convicts share. Wilde juxtaposes the executed man and himself with the line "Yet each man kills the thing he loves". Wilde too was separated from his wife and sons. He adopted the proletarian ballad form and the author was credited as "C33", Wilde's cell number in Reading Gaol. He suggested that it be published in Reynolds' Magazine, "because it circulates widely among the criminal classes – to which I now belong – for once I will be read by my peers – a new experience for me". It was an immediate roaring commercial success, going through seven editions in less than two years, only after which "[Oscar Wilde]" was added to the title page, though many in literary circles had known Wilde to be the author. It brought him a small amount of money.

Although Douglas had been the cause of his misfortunes, he and Wilde were reunited in August 1897 at Rouen. This meeting was disapproved of by the friends and families of both men. Constance Wilde was already refusing to meet Wilde or allow him to see their sons, though she sent him money

– a meagre three pounds a week. During the latter part of 1897, Wilde and Douglas lived together near Naples for a few months until they were separated by their families under the threat of cutting off all funds.

Wilde's final address was at the dingy Hôtel d'Alsace (now known as L'Hôtel), on rue des Beaux-Arts in Saint-Germain-des-Prés, Paris. "This poverty really breaks one's heart: it is so sale [filthy], so utterly depressing, so hopeless. Pray do what you can" he wrote to his publisher. He corrected and published An Ideal Husband and The Importance of Being Earnest, the proofs of which, according to Ellmann, show a man "very much in command of himself and of the play" but he refused to write anything else: "I can write, but have lost the joy of writing".

He wandered the boulevards alone and spent what little money he had on alcohol. A series of embarrassing encounters with English visitors, or Frenchmen he had known in better days, drowned his spirit. Soon Wilde was sufficiently confined to his hotel to joke, on one of his final trips outside, "My wallpaper and I are fighting a duel to the death. One of us has got to go". On 12 October 1900 he sent a telegram to Ross: "Terribly weak. Please come". His moods fluctuated; Max Beerbohm relates how their mutual friend Reginald 'Reggie' Turner had found Wilde very depressed after a nightmare. "I dreamt that I had died, and was supping with the dead!" "I am sure", Turner replied, "that you must have been the life and soul of the party." Turner was one of the few of the old circle who remained with Wilde to the end and was at his bedside when he died.

Death

By 25 November 1900 Wilde had developed meningitis, then called cerebral meningitis. Robbie Ross arrived on 29 November, sent for a priest and Wilde was conditionally baptised into the Catholic Church by Fr Cuthbert Dunne, a Passionist priest from Dublin, Wilde having been baptised in the Church of Ireland and having moreover a recollection of Catholic baptism as a child, a fact later attested to by the minister of the sacrament, Fr Lawrence Fox. Fr Dunne recorded the baptism,

As the voiture rolled through the dark streets that wintry night, the sad story of Oscar Wilde was in part repeated to me... Robert Ross knelt by the bedside, assisting me as best he could while I administered conditional baptism, and afterwards answering the responses while I gave Extreme Unction to the prostrate man and recited the prayers for the dying. As the man was in a semi-comatose condition, I did not venture to administer the Holy Viaticum; still I must add that he could be roused and was roused from this state in my presence. When roused, he gave signs of being inwardly conscious... Indeed I was fully satisfied that he understood me when told that I was about to receive him into the Catholic Church and gave him the Last Sacraments... And when I repeated close to his ear the Holy Names, the Acts of Contrition, Faith, Hope and Charity, with acts of humble resignation to the Will of God, he tried all through to say the words after me.

Wilde died of meningitis on 30 November 1900. Different opinions are given as to the cause of the disease: Richard Ellmann claimed it was syphilitic; Merlin Holland, Wilde's grandson, thought this to be a misconception, noting that Wilde's meningitis followed a surgical intervention, perhaps a mastoidectomy; Wilde's physicians, Dr Paul Cleiss and A'Court Tucker, reported that the condition stemmed from an old suppuration of the right ear (from the prison injury, see above) treated for several years (une ancienne suppuration de l'oreille droite d'ailleurs en traitement depuis plusieurs années) and made no allusion to syphilis.

Burial

Wilde was initially buried in the Cimetière de Bagneux outside Paris; in 1909 his remains were disinterred and transferred to Père Lachaise Cemetery, inside the city. His tomb there was designed by Sir Jacob Epstein. It was commissioned by Robert Ross, who asked for a small compartment to be made for his own ashes, which were duly transferred in 1950. The modernist angel depicted as a relief on the tomb was originally complete with male genitalia, which were initially censored by French Authorities with a golden leaf. The genitals have since been vandalised; their current whereabouts are unknown. In 2000, Leon Johnson, a multimedia artist, installed a silver prosthesis to replace them. In 2011, the tomb was cleaned of the many lipstick marks left there by admirers and a glass barrier was installed to prevent further marks or damage.

The epitaph is a verse from The Ballad of Reading Gaol,

And alien tears will fill for him

Pity's long-broken urn,

For his mourners will be outcast men,

And outcasts always mourn.

Posthumous pardon

In 2017, Wilde was among an estimated 50,000 men who were pardoned for homosexual acts that were no longer considered offences under the Policing and Crime Act 2017. The Act is known informally as the Alan Turing law.

Biographies

Wilde's life has been the subject of numerous biographies since his death. The earliest were memoirs by those who knew him: often they are personal or impressionistic accounts which can be good character sketches, but are sometimes factually unreliable. Frank Harris, his friend and editor, wrote a biography, Oscar Wilde: His Life and Confessions (1916); though prone to exaggeration and sometimes factually inaccurate, it offers a good literary portrait of Wilde. Lord Alfred Douglas wrote two books about his relationship with Wilde. Oscar Wilde and Myself (1914), largely ghost-written by T. W. H. Crosland, vindictively reacted to Douglas's discovery that De Profundis was addressed to him and defensively tried to distance him from Wilde's scandalous reputation. Both authors later regretted their work. Later, in Oscar Wilde: A Summing Up (1939) and his Autobiography he was more sympathetic to Wilde. Of Wilde's other close friends, Robert Sherard; Robert Ross, his literary executor; and Charles Ricketts variously published biographies, reminiscences or correspondence. The first more or less objective biography of Wilde came about when Hesketh Pearson wrote Oscar Wilde: His Life and Wit (1946). In 1954 Wilde's son Vyvyan Holland published his memoir Son of Oscar Wilde, which recounts the difficulties Wilde's wife and children faced after his imprisonment. It was revised and updated by Merlin Holland in 1989.

Oscar Wilde, a critical study by Arthur Ransome was published in 1912. The book only briefly mentioned Wilde's life, but subsequently Ransome (and The Times Book Club) were sued for libel by Lord Alfred Douglas. In April 1913 Douglas lost the libel action after a reading of De Profundis refuted his claims.

Richard Ellmann wrote his 1987 biography Oscar Wilde, for which he posthumously won a National (USA) Book Critics Circle Award in 1988 and a Pulitzer Prize in 1989. The book was the basis for the 1997 film Wilde, directed by Brian Gilbert and starring Stephen Fry as the title character.

Neil McKenna's 2003 biography, The Secret Life of Oscar Wilde, offers an exploration of Wilde's sexuality. Often speculative in nature, it was widely criticised for its pure conjecture and lack of scholarly rigour. Thomas Wright's Oscar's Books (2008) explores Wilde's reading from his childhood in Dublin to his death in Paris. After tracking down many books that once belonged to Wilde's Tite Street library (dispersed at the time of his trials), Wright was the first to examine Wilde's marginalia.

Later on, I think everyone will recognise his achievements; his plays and essays will endure. Of course, you may think with others that his personality and conversation were far more wonderful than anything he wrote, so that his written works give only a pale reflection of his power. Perhaps that is so, and of course, it will be impossible to reproduce what is gone forever.

Robert Ross, 23 December 1900

In 2018, Matthew Sturgis' "Oscar: A Life," was published in London. The book incorporates rediscovered letters and other documents and is the most extensively researched biography of Wilde to appear since 1988.

Parisian literati, also produced several biographies and monographs on him. André Gide wrote In Memoriam, Oscar Wilde and Wilde also features in his journals. Thomas Louis, who had earlier translated books on Wilde into French, produced his own L'esprit d'Oscar Wilde in 1920. Modern books include Philippe Jullian's Oscar Wilde, and L'affaire Oscar Wilde, ou, Du danger de laisser la justice mettre le nez dans nos draps (The Oscar Wilde Affair, or, On the Danger of Allowing Justice to put its Nose in our Sheets) by Odon Vallet, a French religious historian. (Source: Wikipedia)

CPSIA information can be obtained
at www.ICGtesting.com
Printed in the USA
BVHW031027160919
558547BV00008B/176/P